~ My Parents
Went Mac!

An easy guide
to using a Mac computer

Louise Latremouille

My Parents Went Mac

Live with adventure,
for without adventure, there is no learning.

This is for Dad.
We miss you.

www.myparentsfirst.com

Live   Love   Learn

The sale of this book and other books published by KLMK
Enterprises help raise funds for cancer research.
Find a Cure.

Published by KLMK Enterprises, www.myparentsfirst.com
Printed by Hignell Printing, Winnipeg, MB, Canada
Fourth printing, December 2011

ISBN 978-0-9732728-3-3

Welcome

New to a Mac? *My Parents Went Mac* will guide you through the basics with simple step-by-step instructions. Come on along! You'll be enjoying your Mac in no time at all!

I've always felt the easiest way to learn is by doing, so... Let's Get Doing!

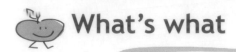

What's what

Macs come in many different shapes and sizes. You may have an older model, or a newer one than we talk about here (lucky you!) but most things will be the same.

iMac

The all-in-one iMac is amazing! Everything, the CD/DVD drive, and all its brains, are tucked in behind a beautiful monitor. It even comes with a built-in camera! A full-sized keyboard and mouse come with it.

MacBooks

MacBooks are lightweight, powerful, talented laptops!

You can use the Trackpad to move your mouse around the screen. Or you can attach and use a regular mouse.

What's what

Mac Pro
Aptly named! Apple's most powerful system is perfect for professionals in the editing and movie business.

The Mac Pro comes with a keyboard, but you have to buy a monitor.

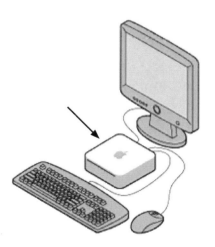

Mac Mini
Mac Mini is a small, very portable, computer. It's just that little unit in the middle of the picture!

Apple calls it a BYODKM. Or, Bring Your Own Display, Keyboard & Mouse!

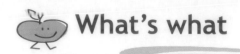
On the side, back or front of your Mac computer you will see a variety of outlets, they are called *Ports.*

You use ports to connect devices to your computer, like a mouse, a printer, a monitor, a camera, an iPod...

Each port is connected to a component inside your Mac. Ports for different types of devices, look different from each other. You will find the locations and types of ports, differ from Mac to Mac.

Here's what the ports look like and what they are for:

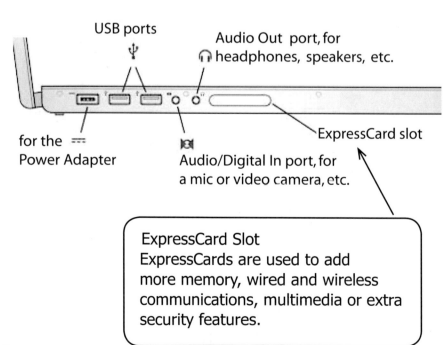

USB ports

Audio Out port, for headphones, speakers, etc.

for the ═ Power Adapter

Audio/Digital In port, for a mic or video camera, etc.

ExpressCard slot

ExpressCard Slot
ExpressCards are used to add more memory, wired and wireless communications, multimedia or extra security features.

USB Port
USB stands for Universal Serial Bus, Universal being the key word. Lots of different devices, from a camera to a mouse, use USB ports to connect to a computer.

Firewire Port
Firewire allows high-speed communication between two computers. It's also what you need to copy a digital video from your computer to another device.

Ethernet Port
An ethernet port is for a high-speed internet connection.

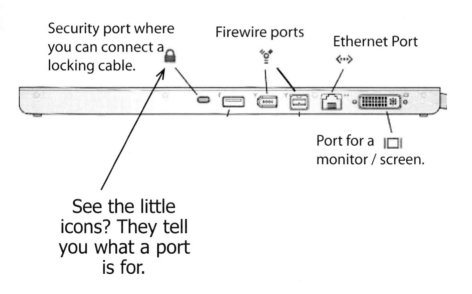

Security port where you can connect a locking cable.

Firewire ports

Ethernet Port

Port for a monitor / screen.

See the little icons? They tell you what a port is for.

What's what

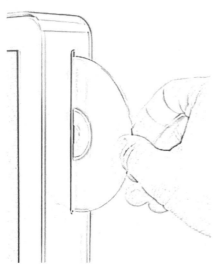

The CD/DVD Drive
Somewhere along the edge of your Mac you will see **the CD/DVD drive**.

It is just a thin opening, the width of a CD.

It's easy to slide a CD or DVD into the drive.

There are a few ways to eject disks!

Here's how to eject disks:

* If your keyboard has an eject key, ▲ press it!

* If you don't have an eject key, press the F12 key.

* If there is a program open that's using the CD, slide your mouse along the headings in the Menu Bar. You will see "Eject Disc" in one of the menus that drop down.

* Look for an icon on your desktop that represents the disc. Click over the icon to see the option "Eject".

* If you see an icon on your desktop that is representing the disc, you can drag the icon to the trash can in the dock. Once there, the trash can will change to an eject icon. Click and the CD should eject, unless the program is still using it.

* If all else fails... restart your Mac, and hold down the mouse click while it's rebooting!

The invention of the computer mouse has made it possible for even the most techno-challenged person to feel like a pro!

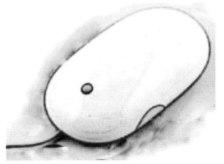

Mighty Mouse

Mac's Mighty Mouse is pretty cool, but any type of mouse will work with your Mac.

The Mouse Pad
When your Mac is all set up, the mouse will rest on one side of the keyboard. Having a mouse pad is not essential, but will help keep your mouse clean and prolong its life. That, and it's nice to have something soft to rest your wrist on!

The Mouse on your Monitor
An arrow, or something like that, will move around on your screen when you move your mouse. They will move together, like great dance partners.

The Mighty Mouse Ball or a Roller?
Most...*mice? (What's the plural for a computer mouse?)*

have a ball or a roller. A mouse roller is a great tool to scroll up and down pages on your computer. What's different between a *roller* and the *ball* on a Mighty Mouse? The ball lets you scroll any which way you want.

Regular Mouse

7

What's what

A little further along, when we're into System Preferences, you'll learn how to personalize how your mouse works!

A friend of mine who is left-handed, has his mouse set up all backwards to what I'm used to. I'm a klutz with his mouse, but it suits him just fine.

Both a regular mouse and a Mighty Mouse left and right click. The Mighty Mouse has a smooth surface, but has touch sensors under the surface that tell it where you're clicking.

The Left-click
If you move the mouse around your screen and left-click, you cursor will instantly arrive at that spot! *The left-click is used for giving commands.*

The Right-click
The right-click is used for getting commands. Try it! Right click your mouse and see a menu pop up.

The Double-click
A double-click will open some things. It's so helpful to know how to do it. The best way I can describe how to do it is with the song *Happy Birthday*. You sing the word *Happy* normally, in one beat. To do a double-click, sing Happy twice in that one beat. *Click to the beat!*

What's what

Mousing Skills!

Highlighting

When you highlight text or objects on your computer screen, you are telling your computer that you want to do something with that particular area.

Here's how to highlight text on a document:

1. Click your mouse at the beginning of the text you want to highlight to move the cursor there.

2. Hold down the left-click button and drag the cursor over the text you want highlighted.

3. Release the button when you're done.

4. The on-screen highlighting is only temporary. It is only active until you tell your Mac what you want to do with it. To remove the highlighting, just move your mouse anywhere on the screen and left-click.

Drag and Drop

Drag and Drop is fantastically easy, and the preferred way to move files, pictures - almost anything, around on a Mac.

1. To highlight a folder, move your mouse over top of it and left-click.

2. Keep holding the left-click down and drag the folder to the location you want to move it to.

3. When you have the file over top of where you want it to go, release the left click.

Drag & Drop, that's it!

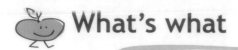

What's what

The keyboard is your typewriter!

Today's Apple keyboards are very
sleek in design.

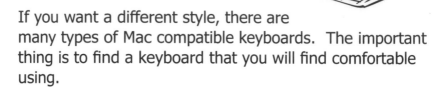

If you want a different style, there are
many types of Mac compatible keyboards. The important
thing is to find a keyboard that you will find comfortable
using.

Keyboards have all the regular typewriter keys *and keys
that are just for a computer.* On the next few pages I'll let
you know about the computer-type keys, using these two
keyboards.

MacBook Keyboard

Apple Keyboard

What's what 🍎

The Apple Keyboard.

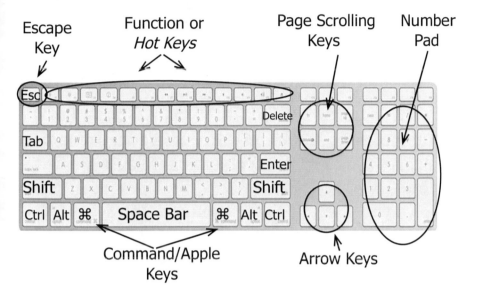

Escape Key

Function or *Hot Keys*

Page Scrolling Keys

Number Pad

Command/Apple Keys

Arrow Keys

Starting at the Escape key, we'll work our way around the keyboard clockwise and learn what keys do what!

What's what:

* The **Escape** key will help you quit or *escape* whatever you are currently doing on you computer.

* The **Hot** keys have great keyboard shortcuts for things like speaker volume, screen brightness and more.

* Use the **Page Scrolling** Keys to look through a document or webpage. Press **Home** and you will instantly go to the beginning of the document; or **End**, to go to the end!.

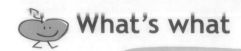
* If you are working with numbers often, using the **Number Key Pad** is the way to go! Rest your middle finger on the 5, and let your fingers do the walking!

* The **Arrow** keys are great for moving your *cursor** one space at a time.

What's a Cursor? It's the blinking line on your computer screen, that tells you where your mouse is active, or where you would type if you were typing!

...not a curser...

* The **Shift** key changes the letters to CAPITALS.

* Use the **Enter** key to finish off a command. It is also a **Return** key, used to go down a line when you're just typing!

* You will see a **Delete forward** key, for deleting forward from where you typed and a **Delete backward** key, for deleting backwards!

* The **Control, Alt & Command** keys work together with other keys, to perform various commands. Commands like copy, paste, quit application, etc.

* The **Space Bar** makes spaces between words!

MacBook keyboard

MacBooks are laptops.

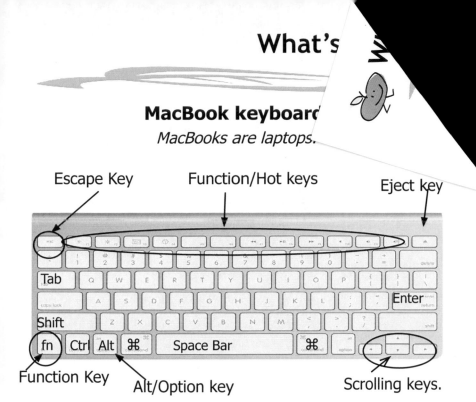

Escape Key   Function/Hot keys   Eject key

Function Key   Alt/Option key   Scrolling keys.

The MacBook keyboard is...*condensed.*

For instance, the number pad seen on the right side of a regular keyboard is part of the lettered keys on a MacBook. 1, 2, & 3 are on J, K, & L. The arrow keys double for regular scrolling keys as well as page scrolling keys.

To activate the number pad, press Num Lock, found on the F6 key. *(Don't forget to turn it off when you don't want that function any more!)*

To use the Arrow keys as Page keys, press them together with the (⌘) Command key!

You might also notice the addition of the Function (fn) key. This is very handy if you want to set up your own shortcuts! You can also use the function key with the delete backwards key to change it to delete forward.

hat's what

Here are the icons (little pictures) on the main part of the keyboard, and what they mean!

Did you notice there are two Command icons? They do the same thing. You might have either or both of these icons on the same key!

The **Command/Apple, Control and Option** keys all work together with other keys to create shortcuts for all sorts of commands.

I've put together a list some common keyboard shortcuts for you, find it on page 163!

The Function keys are now Hot keys!

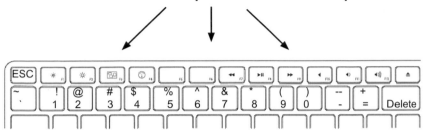

The Function keys have never been much use for us regular people. But now Apple has made them *Hot keys!*

A hot key is a key that has been assigned a shortcut.

You might have these icons on some of the F keys.
Here's what they mean:

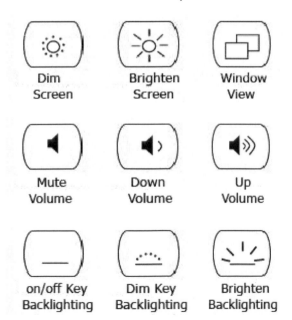

15

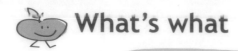

What's what

Use the page scrolling keys
to scan through a document or webpage.

Press *Home* and you will instantly go to the beginning of a document; or *End*, to go to the end!

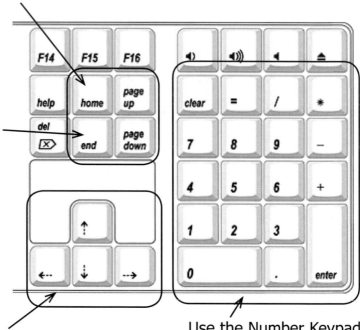

The Arrow keys move your cursor one space at a time.

Use the Number Keypad if you are working with numbers often.
It's the way to go!

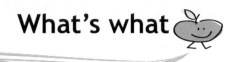

You might have Media keys on your keyboard.

Media keys work with various types of media,
like CD's, DVD's, or even your iPod!

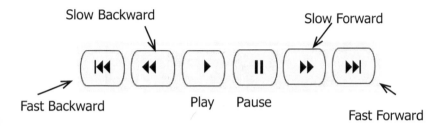

Slow Backward

Slow Forward

Fast Backward

Play   Pause

Fast Forward

And of course, if you are using a CD, DVD or an iPod,
don't forget about the Eject Media key!
It is marked with this symbol: ▲

*Relax! Soon you'll remember
all you need to know...*

Bright Ideas

* _____

* _____

* _____

* _____

* _____

* _____

* _____

* _____

*

*

*

*

*

*

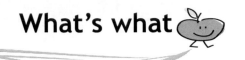

A Desktop,
in computer lingo,
is what you see on your computer screen.

Here is a quick explanation of what's what.

The Menu Bar

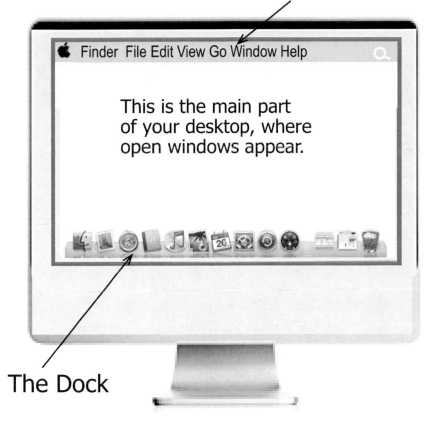

Finder File Edit View Go Window Help

This is the main part
of your desktop, where
open windows appear.

The Dock

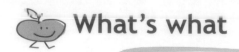 **What's what**

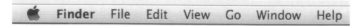

The Menu Bar changes to reflect what program is active.

| 🍎 | **Finder** | File | Edit | View | Go | Window | Help |

When you turn on your Mac, you will see *Finder* along the menu bar. *Finder is always on when your computer is on;* it's a program that helps to manage other programs.

You might have icons in the middle of your desktop that represent programs or folders. Icons are easy to add and can be quick shortcuts to your favorite things!

The Dock has lots of icons. Each icon represents an application, tool, or folder in your Mac. Just click on an icon to open it up.

On the next few pages we'll learn about the Menu Bar and the Dock. Starting with the Dock.....

Mac-Lingo ... Application

When using a Mac you won't often see or hear the word "Program". Apple prefers to call their programs, "Applications".

So... Application = Program!

What's what

The Dock

Any application loaded into your system can have an icon.

Y*our* Dock might have more — or less icons showing.

Apple might change an icon when they update a program or launch a new operating system. I'm using Mac OS X, 10.5.5 and the icons I show reflect that.

Get to know *your* icons!

Remember, to open an application

CLICK ON ITS ICON!

The Dock is organized into two parts. See the faint divider line closer to the right hand side? *It looks like a highway line.* It is separating Application icons from Folder-type icons.

If you add icons to your Dock, keep your Mac happy - keep it organized! Applications to the left. Folders to the right.

Organizing the dock:

 * Drag the icons around on the dock to rearrange them.
 * **To remove an icon**, simply drag it off the dock. Poof!
 * All your programs can be found in Finder. When you open an application from Finder, you will see its icon show up on the dock. To keep it there, move your mouse over top of the icon, right click and choose **"keep in dock"**.

21

 # What's what

Icons and Applications

FINDER
Open Finder to find and open anything in your computer. You can also easily move your files around within Finder. - Drag & drop!

DASHBOARD
The Dashboard holds Widgets. What's a Widget? Widgets are things like a calculator, a weather forecast, a clock, a calendar....

MAIL
This is Apple's email application.

SAFARI
This is Apple's internet browser.

iCHAT
This is Apple's instant messaging application.

ADDRESS BOOK
This is your address book for eMail contacts, and anyone else you want to put in there!

iTUNES
iTunes is Apple's music program. Works by itself or with an iPod.

iPHOTO
This is Apple's photo program. It works with digital cameras and is SO very easy to use!

What's what

Icons and Applications

iMOVIE
Plug your video camera into your Mac and iMovie will come alive! It's super easy to download and edit videos.

iDVD
Use iDVD to burn videos and pictures onto a DVD. Great for slideshows too!

GARAGE BAND
This is your own personal music studio! Record and mix live music or create music with virtual instruments.

PAGES
Pages is Apple's word processing application. It is similar to *Microsoft Word*.

NUMBERS
This is Apple's spreadsheet application. It is similar to *Microsoft Excel*.

KEYNOTE
With Keynote you will be able to create wonderful presentations. Keynote is comparable to *Power Point*.

iWEB
With iWeb you can create your own websites.

What's what

Icons and Applications

iCAL
iCal is a calendar (and a Widget!). Very handy to organize your days!

PHOTO BOOTH
If your Mac has a built-in camera you will have Photo Booth to use and play with. It's fun!

SYSTEM PREFERENCES
This is where you can personalize your Mac. Make it look and respond the way you want!

Older Macs might have this icon for System Preferences.

TIME MACHINE
This is a backup system.

DOCUMENTS
When you create new documents they will be saved into this folder.

DOWNLOADS
This is where the files you save from the internet go.

TRASH
Last but never least, the trash can! Any item you delete from your system will land in the trash can.

Bright Ideas

* _____
* _____
* _____
* _____
* _____
* _____
* _____
* _____
*
*
*
*
*
*

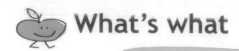

What's what

The Menu Bar.

You are going to love this Bar! Find it neatly tucked at the top of your desktop screen, with the Apple logo on the left hand side.

The left side of the bar shows the Application Menus. The headings change to suit whatever program is most active. By default, *Finder* is there when everything else is closed.

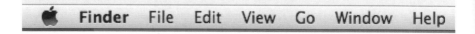

The right hand side of the Menu Bar shows icons for a few of iStat menus (system tools) found in your Mac.

These are pretty standard iStat menus, the icons showing on your Mac might be different. You can change what iStat icons are showing through System Preferences, under Other.

It's easy to find out what an icon is for — just click on it!

What's what 🍎

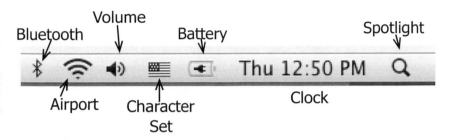

Bluetooth
Volume
Battery
Spotlight
Airport
Character Set
Clock

iStat menus: Here's what they do!

Bluetooth	*Bluetooth* is wireless technology. If you have a wireless mouse or keyboard, it may communicate with your computer using Bluetooth technology.
Airport	This an indicator for wireless internet. If you are connected to the internet some other way, like with an ethernet cable, the ethernet cable icon would show up here.
Volume	Click here to see the volume level that is set on your speakers.
Character Set	Don't mess with this! Character Set is telling your computer what language you are using and how the letters and numbers should look for your language.
Battery	If you have a portable computer, click here to see the charge level in your battery.
Clock	If you like, you can change the clock to look like an analog clock.
Spotlight	Spotlight can search for anything in your computer. Click your mouse over this icon and a small window opens; type in what you are looking for.

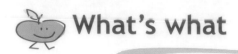 # What's what

The Menu Bar - and Applications

🍎 **iCal** File Edit Calendar View Window Help

When you open an application the left side of the menu bar changes to match that application.

It's easier to learn by doing, so....

Let's Practice!

Click on the iCal icon

and open it up!

An application's window might be off by itself, separate from the Menu Bar.

Windows can be moved around and re-sized.

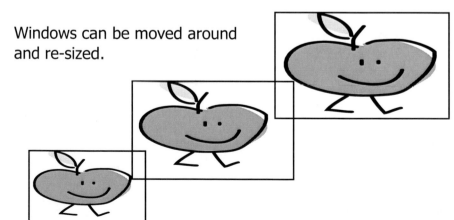

What's what

Have a look at the menu bar. Notice that it says *iCal* beside the Apple logo, and that the headings have changed to suit iCal.

Menu bar headings change to suit whatever window is active!

Desktop Background   Menu bar   Active Window

Re-size corner

To move a window around on your desktop:

1. Move your mouse over the top part of the window. (On the bar where the 3 circles are.)

2. Hold the mouse click down and move the window around!

29

What's what

You can re-size a window if you see this little striped triangle in the bottom right corner.

To re-size an active window:

push
&
pull

1. Click and hold your mouse down over this corner.
2. With your mouse still clicked down, move it around. The window will re-size with you!

Try it - Let's keep practicing!

Open another application on Dock. It doesn't matter what. Notice how the windows open up on top of each other.

The window for the active application seems to float on top of other windows that are open in the background. The active window is also brighter than other windows. Look how the menu bar changes with each different application. Click on a different window to make it active and bring it to the front.

You can have many windows open at one time!

What's what

Before we go on...
I should mention about these three circles! They
Close, Reduce and Expand
windows.

Red   Amber   Green

These circles are on the **top left corner** of **open windows**.
NOT on the menu bar... ON the open windows!

Here's what they do:

 This will CLOSE the window.

 This will SHRINK the window onto the right side
of your dock. Click on the application's icon to
enlarge it again.

 Click on this once, and the window will expand to
the whole size of your screen. Click on it again,
and the window will be smaller again.

Good to know...
These circles don't close a program, just the window.
**The easiest way to close a program is to
press these keys together: ⌘ + Q**
That's the Control key + the letter Q for quit!

Bright Ideas

* _____

* _____

* _____

* _____

* _____

* _____

* _____

* _____

*

*

*

*

*

*

Customize

It's nice to get things
just the way you like them!

Customize

Customize

Customizing your Mac
is the best first step to getting to know and enjoy it.
With just a little tweaking,
your Mac will respond the way you want it to!

Find all the tools to customize your system in System Preferences!

Let's do this together!

Find the System Preferences icon
on the dock. Click on it to open it up.

I have the operating system "Leopard" on my Mac and the graphics I show reflect that. If you have a different system on your Mac, things might look just a little different. Don't worry though, you will be able to follow along!

I'm not going to hold your hand for every step. Once you know what the tool is and what it does, personalizing the setting to the way you want is very straight forward. Really!

Ready?   Let's go!

TIP! When you make a change in System
Preferences the effect is immediate. If
you don't like what you changed, the
tool is still open and it's so easy to
undo what you just did. No worries!

Customize

This is the System Preferences window.

Notice how it's divided into rows.

Each row has items that are related to each other.

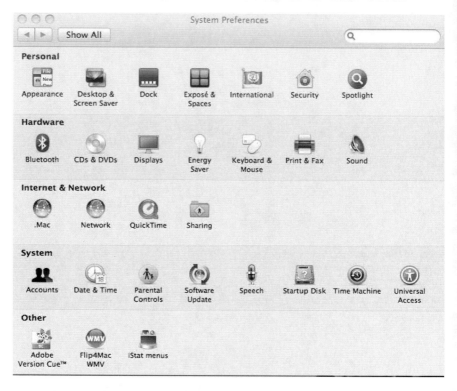

Good to know...
When you have an item open,
and you want to go back to this screen,
click on the "Show All" button. It is always there.

"Show All" brings you back to this window.

Customize

*It's nice getting things
just the way you want them!*

Remember. To open an item, just click on the icon.

Personal Preferences

The top row is labeled *Personal*. These tools will help you
set up how your desktop looks and acts.

Appearance
In Appearance you can change the colors in the menus,
buttons and windows, as well as how the *scroll bar* reacts.

The scroll bar is the slidey bar found along the
side and bottom of most windows.
To slide the Scroll bar, move your mouse
pointer over it, hold down the left-click on your
mouse, and move it!
Easy like pie!

Customize

Appearance, continued

Number of Recent Items - I like the Documents set to 5. When you open files, their names are kept in a Recent Items submenu in the Apple menu. This is a great tool for finding and opening the files again!

Font smoothing style - I leave mine at Automatic. I figure my Mac knows best!

Desktop & Screen Saver

In Desktop you can set the picture that is on your computer screen when everything is closed.

A Screen Saver starts when your computer is idle. Screen Savers used to be important to the life of your monitor, not any more. Nowadays they are more entertaining.

Click around on the different options; see how easy it it to personalize these settings.

Dock

Play with this until you get the Dock to look and act the way you want it to. *Tip... If your Dock has disappeared and you are wondering where it is... Look here and see if "Automatically hide and show the Dock" is ticked!*

Exposé and Spaces

If you have many windows open, they will look layered over each other. Use Exposé to get a quick *thumbnail* view of all the windows that are open.

Spaces can help you organize your desktop and files.

Customize

International
<u>Language:</u> This is very cool — especially if you are multi-lingual! You will see a list that has many languages. Put your preferred language at the top.

<u>Formats:</u> Time Zone, Region, Currency... Setting things up in here can save you a lot of frustration in the future. Don't be afraid to click around; you're not going to break it!

<u>Input Menu:</u> **Be afraid here!** Unless you know what you are doing, don't mess with this setting.

Security
Click through the headings, General, File Vault & Firewall. Set the security levels to whatever you are comfortable with. Remember, if you decide to use passwords, write them down somewhere in case you forget them....

Spotlight
Spotlight is a super search tool. In System Preferences, you can set the order that search results appear, and where your computer will look for things. If everything is checked, Spotlight will look everywhere for whatever it is you're looking for.

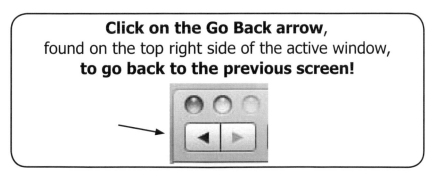

Click on the Go Back arrow,
found on the top right side of the active window,
to go back to the previous screen!

Customize

Hardware Settings

Hardware

Bluetooth · CDs & DVDs · Displays · Energy Saver · Keyboard & Mouse · Print & Fax · Sound

Hardware in a computer means things that you can actually touch. The display screen, the disk drive, the keyboard, even a computer chip, are all considered hardware.

Software is needed to program hardware!

Bluetooth
Bluetooth is a wireless technology that your Mac can really jive with! If you have other devices that are Bluetooth enabled, your Mac will be looking for them. When you set up a wireless device (maybe a printer or a mouse) follow the simple steps to set it up.

CD's & DVD's
How great is it that you can set up your Mac to work just the way you want it to — all the way down to what happens when you insert a CD (music) or a DVD (movie). Click and choose the options you want.

Click on the Go Forward arrow,
found on the top right side of the active window,
to go forward... *if you went back!*

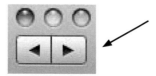

Customize

Hardware

Bluetooth   CDs & DVDs   Displays   Energy Saver   Keyboard & Mouse   Print & Fax   Sound

Displays

Display and Color

Click on these to see how your monitor is configured. If everything looks right on your screen, don't muck with the settings! You might even want to note down what the settings are... in case someone else mucks with them.

I really like, "Automatically adjust brightness as ambient light changes." It is so cool that the screen's brightness can magically adjust to how much light is in the room!

Energy Saver

This is where you tell your computer, or even just the monitor, to automatically *sleep* when you're not using it. Adjust the settings to your preferences. It's so easy to do!

Customize

Keyboard and Mouse
Lots of options here to make your mouse and keyboard work the way your want them to.

Depending on how you type, *or mouse,* making adjustments here could make a world of difference to you.

For instance if you are a very slow typist, under the Keyboard tab, set the *key repeat rate* to slow; if you type like lightning — set it to fast!

Trackpad
If you have a laptop you will see Trackpad. The trackpad is right below your keyboard and works like a mouse.

Mouse
Move your mouse around while you make these adjustments. You will easily be able to get the mouse to react the way you expect it to.

If you are using Mac's Mighty Mouse, you'll see lots of other cool tools here too!

Customize

Bluetooth

Remember, Bluetooth is a wireless technology. If you have either a Bluetooth enabled mouse or keyboard, you'll set up the defaults here.

Keyboard Shortcuts

Macs have great keyboard shortcuts. If you do the same *mouse task* over and over again, creating a keyboard shortcut to do that task might just be the thing for you!

You'll find all the pre-programed shortcuts in the tab that opens up. To make your own shortcuts in your favorite application, click on the **+** sign and follow the directions.

Print & Fax

If you have a printer or a fax machine connected to your Mac, you will see its information here.

When you connect a new printer, you can add that printer's info to your Mac. Just click on the **+** sign and follow the steps!

Your Mac will search to see if it already has your printer's driver to load the printer, or will ask you to insert a disk for the driver.

Wondering what a driver is? Find out next!

Customize

Learning about drivers is a little off the beaten path here, but now seems like the right time to talk about them!

Each device attached to your computer is driven by a *Driver*.

You don't really have to know much about drivers, but a bit of knowledge can make understanding things easier!

The main brain in a computer is its Operating System (OS). The Mac OS is like the conductor to an orchestra. The conductor doesn't have to know how to play the bassoon, piano or drums, but he has to know how to make them all work together!

Operating systems work in a very generic language. Every device speaks in its own secret language, I guess maybe to protect brand technology.

Between the device and your computer a translator, so to speak, is needed.

Bonjour = Hello
Hello = Bonjour

Devices, like printers or cameras, should come with their own driver as part of their installation disk. If you don't have an installation disk, and your Mac can't find a driver for your new device, you might have to download a driver from the internet.

Customize

Sound
This is where you set the Sound Effects — like a little ping when a new email arrives!

Output
Does your Mac have built-in speakers, or external ones? You'll find all the information you need about your speakers here, as well as how to adjust the balance.

Input
This is where you set the levels for a microphone.

Karaoke anyone?

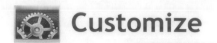

Customize

Internet and Network

Internet & Network

| .Mac | Network | QuickTime | Sharing |

.Mac is now called *Mobile Me*

Mobile Me is an Apple.com web service you can pay for. It costs between $100 to $200 annually, for individual or family subscriptions.

Mobile Me web services include:

* Webmail: yourname@mac.com or yourname@me.com
* An on-line photo gallery to upload your photos,
* A seamless integration with iWeb. iWeb is Mac's website building application.
* All your web devices will sync with each other. For instance, emails are sent to all your devices, not just your work computer or just your iPhone.

Network

Like most screens in your Mac, once you open this screen it is very simple to understand. If you are connected to the internet, there will be a green dot beside where it says how you are connected, as well as the word "connected"!

More importantly, if you are having trouble with your internet connection, this is where you would look to try and fix it!

QuickTime

QuickTime is Apple's amazing multi-platform, multi-media software. When you download a movie from the net, you'll view it with QuickTime.

Customize

Sharing
Macs love to share! Sharing means that other computers can access your computer.

This is a good thing for lots of different reasons. For instance, you might need some help doing something with your Mac and you have a Mac Guru friend who can help you! By enabling *screen sharing*, your Mac Guru friend will see what's on your screen and even work with your files! Be careful though, share with only those you really TRUST.

System Settings

Accounts
Find your log-in and password settings here. The main account, or *log-in screen* is always the Admin account. If you don't need a password every time you open your computer, use the Admin account and leave the Password blank.

If you want to use **Parental Controls** you have to use a password for your Admin account. You will also have to create Guest Accounts for your kids to log onto your Mac, then click on "Enable Parental Controls" to set your preferences.

Customize

Date & Time
You can change everything to do with the clock here. If you choose "Announce the time", you have to enable "Speech". *Speech is coming up!*

Parental Controls
I just talked about this under "Accounts", so instead of repeating myself... *go back a page!*

Software Update
It is VERY important to keep your system up-to-date. Set how often you want your system to check for, and download updates. I'd recommend at least once a week.

Speech
Let your Mac talk to you! Play around with these settings, it's fun!

Startup Disk
Literally. This is the system disk that your Mac uses when it starts up. *If you are using Leopard, you can start up as a Mac or choose to use Microsoft Windows! Really!*

You can also choose a system disk when your computer is booting. Just after you turn it on, when the screen is still blank, press the Alt/Option key. The startup disks will show up. To open the operating system you want, click over the startup disk icon, then the arrow below it.

Time Machine
Time Machine helps you backup your files. Backing up files is like having a safety net if your Mac's hard drive gets damaged. A hard drive is where all your information is stored. All your files are on the hard drive, and a backup is a copy of those files.

You can either backup your files to a dedicated area of your hard drive — or you can buy a separate little hard drive (a backup unit), the latter being the much safer and easier way! Here's the scoop on these two ways:

Build a Partition
Partition = Great Wall of China. Well maybe not quite, but partitions split your hard drive into separate areas. You can then dedicate one of the areas for saving backups to. Nice because it's all in your computer, but if the whole hard drive gets fried, you still might lose everything. If you choose to go this way, find a clever computer friend to create the partition for you!

Buy a Backup Hard Drive
Backup hard drives can cost between $100 to $300. A good investment if it's critical you don't lose information. When you buy a Backup hard drive, look on the box and **make sure that it is Mac compatible.** If it is, bring it home and connect it to your computer via a USB port. Your Mac will help you with the rest!

Don't you just ♥ your Mac!

Customize

Universal Access
These are great tools designed to help you if your physical abilities are challenged.

The headings are; Sight, Hearing, Keyboard, Mouse & Trackpad. Each one offers options that might help you.

You will also see the option here that will enable access to *Assistive Devices*.

Other

What shows up here will depend on the programs *you* have in *your* Mac. These are the icons under Other, on my Mac.

iStat menus
Remember when I explained about the right side of the Menu Bar and all those icons? This is where you can choose what you want to see there.

Internet know-how!

Internet know-how!

Knowing just a little
about how the internet works
can make using it a whole lot easier!

AND I LIKE EASY!

*Safari is Apple's internet browser,
but before we dive into it...*

Please, take a wee bit of time
to look over the next couple of pages.

For easy reference, you will see
new words or terms in bold print;
their definitions are together
at the end of each page or section.

Internet know-how

Needs & Wants!

There are different ways to hook up to the internet. Each technology offers something a little different.

Computers need a modem to connect to the internet. Modems convert computer data into the type of data that can travel through the internet.

What type of modem you need is determined by how you will hook up.

How you will hook up is determined by what is available in your area and how fast you want your connection to be.

And when it comes to the internet,

there is definitely a need for speed!

Macs come with built in hardware that makes it easy to connect to the internet, either by wireless or with an **ethernet cable**.

Internet know-how

Here's a bit about internet connections.

High-speed Cable
You need a cable modem to access the internet via *TV cable*. This type of internet connection is very fast, running generally at 2 **mbps**.

Your cable company should provide you with a *cable modem* when you hook up with them as your Internet Service Provider *(ISP)*.

A cable modem is always hooked into the internet and ready for your computer to go on-line. An ethernet cable is used to connect this type of modem to a computer.

DO NOT USE A TELEPHONE CABLE, IT WON'T WORK.

DSL *(a very high speed connection)*
DSL, a *Digital Subscriber Line* is a specially dedicated type of phone line. This is an incredibly fast connection, downloading as fast as 32 **mbps**! A DSL modem, like a cable modem, is always hooked into the internet and ready for your computer to go on-line.

DSL is often referred to as *last mile technology*, because it must be within 3 kilometers *(1.8 miles...)* from a special switching station that is set up along the phone lines. Where available, this technology is offered by telephone companies.

Internet know-how

Wireless

Macs love to go wireless!
A wireless device actually uses technology similar to cell phones. Airports and many public places offer wireless access (Wi-Fi) to the internet. Be aware that this technology offers the least amount of security or privacy.

If you have a high speed internet connection, you can set up a home wireless network. You'll have to buy a wireless broadband router, that you'll connect to your high-speed modem.

When you set up a home wireless network, you can create a password to connect, for extra security.

Modem

A **modem** is the piece of equipment a computer needs to access the internet via phone lines. A modem can be inside a computer or be a separate external unit, like the Apple USB Modem.

The Apple USB Modem connects at 56,700 **bps**. With this type of modem, you can plug directly into your existing phone line. Know that if you use your phone line to access the internet, when you are *on-line,* your phone line is busy.

Connect a regular phone line into one end of the Apple USB Modem, and the other end into a USB port on your Mac.

> *Dial-up internet service,*
> *is the slowest type of internet connection.*

Internet know-how

D e f i n i t i o n s

Modem
Short for modulator-demodulator. It converts regular analog data that normally goes through your phone line to digital data for computer talk and vise-versa. A modem is the piece of equipment needed to access the internet via regular phone lines.

Bps
Bits per second. Bps refers to the speed of information being sent through a modem, to or from the internet. *It takes 8 bits to represent one digit, letter or keystroke!*

56,700bps = fast   2,400bps = slow

Mbps
Mega bits per second. Mega means 1 million. High-speed internet connections deal with mbps and *high-speed connections sure seem a million times faster than dial-up!*

ISP
Internet **S**ervice **P**rovider. This is the company that you pay for internet access and service.

Server
A server is the ISP's *computer.* A server acts as the middleman (computer) between you and the internet.

Ethernet Cable
An ethernet cable transfers data between a high speed modem and a computer.

How to hook-up

Getting hooked up is really as simple as making a phone call and asking about availability and cost.

Here's the scoop on the **who** and **how**, with **what** type of connection you might choose.

For Dial-up Service

Most telephone companies offer internet service. They have a large computer that acts as a server, communicating between you and the rest of the internet. *Any company can offer you internet service, as long as they have the equipment.*

Make sure the ISP you choose is reputable.

A modem connects to a server with a telephone number that has been programmed into your computer. It is important that your server's telephone number is LOCAL to you, or you will have long-distance charges every time you dial up.

Each time you dial up, the server will then look for other settings in your computer confirming that you are a client of theirs, such as access and account codes, etc.

Your ISP should either send a technician out to your home and configure all the settings for you, or offer telephone assistance when you set it up yourself.

DSL

Digital Subscriber Lines are available through telephone companies. Currently DSL is only available in limited areas. Call your local telephone company to see if it is available in your area.

The company that connects you with DSL should provide and install any extra equipment your computer might need, such as a special type of modem that can handle very high speeds. A technician will come to hook up and configure the computer for you. Be sure to ask if this is included in the connection fees.

Wireless service in your home

If you have a high-speed internet connection, you can set up a home wireless network. You'll have to buy a Wireless Broadband Router, that you'll connect to your high-speed modem.

Your ISP might provide wireless service, or include a wireless broadband router when you hook up with them.

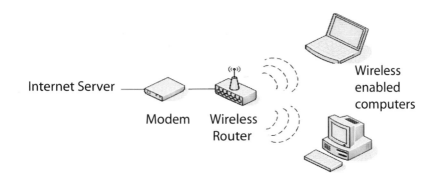

Internet Server

Modem   Wireless Router

Wireless enabled computers

Internet know-how

Cable

Where the technology is available, this is provided through your cable TV company. Call your local cable company to see if high-speed internet service is in your neighborhood!

The cable company should send out a technician to install the extra wiring required, hook up the new cable modem, install any new equipment your computer might need and configure your system to work with their server.

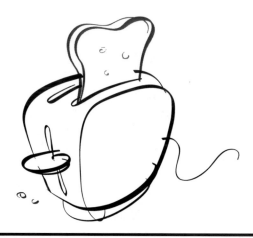

TIP
With Cable, like DSL, your internet line is always active, but that does not mean your computer has to be on-line.

You can work off-line as well.

Think of it like your toaster... it's always plugged in and ready to go, but unless you push the button it is just sitting there!

Internet know-how

Some things are common to all the hook-up methods. You should consider these:

The hook-up or installation fees
Some companies will offer free hook-up with a guarantee of your business for a term. Others will charge a fee. Be sure to ask what is included and shop around.

Included email service
Most ISP's offer email, but you should confirm that yours does! You will want to know what is included and if there are *size restrictions* on files or mail you can send or receive.

Spam
Another consideration is the company's policy on **spam** — internet junk mail. If you don't want it, make sure you can block it!

Companies can charge for internet service in a variety of ways.

Here are some examples:

* *Unlimited Use* for a set monthly fee. This might range from $20 to $100 per month — or more!

* *Hourly Use* for an hourly charge

* Some number of *"free" hours* per month, with *additional charges* for time used beyond those.

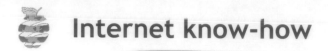
Internet & Mail Settings!

Configuring a computer sounds intimidating. It's not, especially with a Mac!

The first time you connect to the internet, or open Mail, your Mac will walk you through setting it up.

When you configure a program, you're telling it where to go and how to find information in your computer. The first time you connect to a new Internet Service Provider, your Mac needs a bit of information.

Your ISP's **Server** needs to be able to identify your computer, and your Mac needs to be able to find your server.

This is the information your ISP will provide you with and what your Mac needs to connect:

* Your server's **hostname**

* Your **password** and **user name**

* If you are using dial-up, your server's phone number

* **POP** or **IMAP** and **SMTP settings**
  (don't you love acronyms!)

* Your **Server's account type**

Internet know-how

Definitions

Protocol or "P"

You will see the word *protocol* often, or at least a "P" at the end of an acronym. Protocols have enabled the internet to work world wide. Protocols are rules that computers use to communicate. They make it possible for computers all over the world to work together!

Server Type

What type of protocol your server uses. If your server uses a POP protocol, your answer might look like this:

pop.yourservername.com

User Name

A user name can be assigned to you by your server, or you may be able to pick your own. It will often end up being your email address name.

Name

Your real name. This will identify you with your email name.

Port

Ports are the outlets on your Mac. There is an ethernet port on your Mac to connect an ethernet cable to.

SMTP (Simple Mail Transfer Protocol)
The protocol used for sending (outgoing) email.

POP (Post Office Protocol)
  or
IMAP (Internet Message Access Protocol)
Both of these are for retrieving (incoming) email messages.
Your server will use one format or the other.

In the window where you are asked for server information,
your answers for sending and retrieving mail might look like
this:

Outgoing mail

- smtp.nameofyourserver.com

Incoming mail

- pop.nameofyourserver.com
  or
- imap.nameofyourserver.com

You are telling your computer what type of protocol your
server prefers. For retrieving email POP is the most
common; IMAP is a newer version that is a little faster.

*Protocols are rules the
Internet lives by.
Protocols let computers all
over the world speak the same
language and work together!*

Internet know-how

It's a good idea to write down of some of the information your Internet Service Provider will give you.

Your username_____

Your password_____
Passwords should be confidential
Maybe, just write down a password hint here.

Your email address _____

SMTP _____

POP_____

IMAP_____

Your ISP_____

ISP Help Phone #_____

Type of internet connection _____

Internet connection password _____
 (or a hint!)

Bright Ideas

* _____

* _____

* _____

* _____

* _____

* _____

* _____

* _____

*

*

*

*

*

*

Safari

Welcome to the information highway.
You are going to enjoy this Safari!

Safari

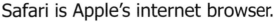

Safari is Apple's internet browser.

An internet browser is a program that finds and displays websites.

Click on the Safari icon to open it up.

The Menu Bar along the top will change to Safari

 Safari File Edit View History Bookmarks Window Help

and a Safari window will open on your Desktop.

My Parents First Computer Guides

http://www.myparentsfirst.com/   Q▾ Google

Google Maps   http://www....sfirst.com/   Apple   Wikipedia

View webpages in this window.

The internet is a wonderful source of information. On the next few pages, you'll discover why so many people use the internet. *It's easy to navigate and fun to use!*

I might not have to say this, but...
you must be connected
to the internet to surf the net.

Safari

What's what on the Safari toolbar.

The bar along the top of the Safari window, *or any application's window,* is called a Toolbar.

Safari's Toolbar has *tools* for surfing websites. What I show above is Apple's default set-up, but you can customize it to your liking. Here's how:

1. Right click your mouse over a gray area in the toolbar. "Customize Toolbar" will appear

2. Move your mouse over top of "*Customize Toolbar"* and click again. This window will open up:

3. To put a Tool on your Toolbar, click and hold your mouse down over an icon. Then, literally, drag it to where you want it. *Drag & Drop!*
   Mac icons LOVE to be DRAGGED!

Safari

Safari Toolbar

◄ ► Back/Fwd	If you are surfing websites, click on the Back arrow to backtrack to previous sites - or Forward if you went Back!
✕ Stop/Reload	If a website is taking too long to "load", you can click on this to stop it. After you click on it, it changes to Reload. **↻** Click Reload to refresh a site.
✄ Open in Dashboard	Dashboard is for Widgets. What's a Widget? Click F12 (or F4 if you have an aluminum keyboard) and see your widgets! *Cool, eh!*
+ Add Bookmark	Bookmarks offer quick access to your favorite websites. Click on this to add a site to your Bookmarks. *More on Bookmarks on page 89.*
⌂ Home	Home is the website that opens when you start Safari. It can be any website you want!
✎ AutoFill	AutoFill helps you fill in personal information in forms on websites. It works together with your Address Book.
A A Text Size	Need larger text on a website? Click on the big A to go bigger, and the small A to go smaller!
🖶 Print	If you are hooked up to a printer, click here to print the webpage you're on.
🐜 Report Bug	If you are having a problem using Safari, like webpages or features not loading right, you can submit the problem to Apple.

Safari

A Web Address

In the middle of the toolbar you'll see the website address window.

A website address is also known as a **URL**, which stands for Uniform Resource Locator.

There are three parts to a URL. The first part is the prefix. It tells your server what type of protocol it uses.

* **http://** is what you will see for most websites. http means Hypertext Transfer Protocol.

* **https://** is what you will see if you are on a secure site. Secure sites use sophisticated encryption that is 99.9% impossible for hackers to get into.

* **ftp://** is what you will see if you are downloading from a site, or adding information to a site. ftp means File Transfer Protocol.

The second part of the address is called the domain name. People often only say this part of the address, omitting the prefix. That's okay because your server can often figure the prefix out for itself.

The third part of an address tells you what type of site it is, such as for commercial intent or from the government.

The different parts of a web address are divided by periods, they are referred to as ***dot***.

http://www.nameofthesite.com

Prefix   Domain Name   Suffix

The suffix gives you an idea of what type of webpage it is.

Here are some examples:

.com	Commercial Business
.ca	Canada
.edu	Educational Institution
.gov	Government Agency
.mil	Military
.net	Network Organization
.org	Organization (non-profit)

Domain names are generally all in lower case (no capital letters) and never ever have spaces in between words.

Safari

A website's **home page** is like a cover to a book. A small website might only have a home page.

When you look at a web address, the three parts in the beginning of the address are *Home.*

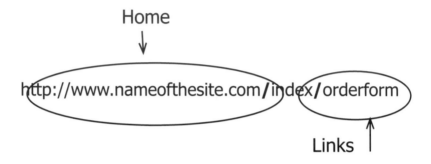

Home

http://www.nameofthesite.com/index/orderform

Links

On a web address, links within a website are separated by slashes at the end of the home address. Links are pages within that website.

Often you will see LOTS of slashes and links at the end of an address. The larger the site, the more links (pages within pages) there will be!

The Menu Bar

 Safari File Edit View History Bookmarks Window Help

Each heading along the Menu Bar has a drop-down menu. On the next few pages we'll learn what's what! Starting with the File menu...

The best way to learn

is by doing.

So open up Safari and www.myparentsfirst.com

Come on, follow along!

Safari

The File Menu

Click on a heading to see the commands in its drop-down menu.

File Edit View History Bookmarks		
New Window	⌘	N
New Tab	⌘	T
Open File	⌘	O
Open Location	⌘	L
Close Window	⌘	W
Close Tab		
Save As...	⌘	S
Mail Contents of this page	⌘	I
Mail Link to this page	⇧ ⌘	I
Open in Dashboard		
Import Bookmarks		
Export Bookmarks		
Print....	⌘	P

Keyboard shortcuts for the commands

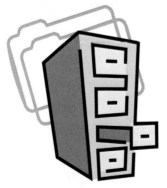

New Window

Instead of leaving a website to go to another, you can open a new window. This is great if you want to look at different websites simultaneously.

File Edit View History Bookmarks	
New Window	⌘ N
New Tab	⌘ T
Open File	⌘ O
Open Location	⌘ L
Close Window	⌘ W
Close Tab	
Save As...	⌘ S
Mail Contents of this page	⇧⌘ I
Mail Link to this page	⌘ I
Open in Dashboard	
Import Bookmarks	
Export Bookmarks	
Print....	⌘ P

New Tab

I love tabs! Instead of having a whole new window for another website, you can have many sites open within the same window! Try it and you'll see what I mean.

* Click on New Tab, or ⌘T. You'll see an "untitled" tab and a blank page open.

* Type an address in the address bar. For example, www.google.com. See how the tab now has the website's title. The site will stay open, even when you go to another tab! Click on the tab to go to that website.

Open File

Use this to open files in your computer. When you're using Safari, this will only open the type of files Safari can open, like picture or html files.

Open Location

This will free up the web address area in the Toolbar, letting you type in a new web address.

Close Window

Closes the Safari window, but leaves the application open. Notice Safari is still along the Menu Bar. ⌘Q quits the application.

Safari

File	Edit	View	History	Bookmarks	
New Window					⌘ N
New Tab					⌘ T
Open File					⌘ O
Open Location					⌘ L
Close Window					⌘ W
Close Tab					
Save As...					⌘ S
Mail Contents of this page					⇧⌘ I
Mail Link to this page					⌘ I
Open in Dashboard					
Import Bookmarks					
Export Bookmarks					
Print....					⌘ P

Close Tab

Close Tab will be greyed out if you don't have a tab open. If there was a Tab open it would be an option to use.

Save As...

Use this to save a website to a folder in your computer. Websites are saved as html files.

Mail Contents of This Page

Use this to email a website to a friend. Warning — this tool sends the page as you see it and it might be too large to download if your friend doesn't have high speed internet.

Mail Link to This Page

This tool will also create a new email, only this time you will only see a link to the site, not the site itself.

A link will look just like the web address that you see in the address bar. When the receiver clicks on the link, their browser will open to that site!

Emailing a link to a website is often a better way to go.

Open in Dashboard

This will let you take a clip (like a lttle snapshot) of part of a website, and make it part of your Dashboard.

Here's a little about the Dashboard

The Dashboard holds "Widgets". Apple Widgets are things like a clock, a weather forecast, a calculator, a dictionary, etc.

You can turn a small part of a website into one of your own dashboard widgets. Here's how:

1. With the website open, click on Open in Dashboard.

2. The site will become shadowed, and with a lit box you will be able to choose what part of the site you want to capture.

3. Once you are over what you want, left-click to create a frame.

4. Look to the top of the webpage and click on Add.

That's it!

Import Bookmarks...   Export Bookmarks....

You can have more than one web browser on a computer. If you do, this will let you import the bookmarks from one browser into another. Vice versa for exporting!

Print...

Prints the website! Best part of this tool is that you can preview what you are going to print before you print it!

The Edit Menu

Edit	View	History	Bookmarks		
Undo				⌘	Z
Redo				⌘	Z
Cut				⌘	X
Copy				⌘	C
Paste				⌘	V
Delete					
Select All			⇧	⌘	A
Auto Fill Form				⌘	A
Find				▶	
Spelling & Grammar				▶	
Special Characters			⌥	⌘	T

Undo and Redo

Ever wish you could undo what you have just done?

Finally your wish is granted!

If you have typed something you don't like, click on Undo to undo it! *Ooops,* maybe it was right? Click on Redo, and what was there will come right back!

You'll find Undo and Redo

under Edit in almost every program.

If you want to copy, cut or delete something, you must **highlight it** first!

You have to tell your computer what you are selecting to edit.

* To select text, use your cursor to highlight it.

* To select a picture, click your mouse over it.

Cut, Copy, Paste and Delete

These four editing tools are what make using a computer so terrific! Get to know how to use them. You can even copy something from one program and paste it into another!

Cut and Delete
Cut and Delete sound like the same thing, but there is a difference!

 Choose to **Delete** something and it will either disappear (if it's just text) or go to your trash can.

Choose to **Cut** something and it goes to the "clipboard".

The clipboard is like a holding tank for items you would like to paste later.

Most programs will only hold one item at a time on the clipboard. If you "cut" another item, it will replace whatever was on the clipboard before.

Remember about Undo,
if you delete something you don't want to!

Safari

Copy and Paste

It's way easier to learn by doing, so let's copy something from a website onto a blank document.

1. First open a blank document. Here's a couple of options:

   * Open your email program, and then a New Message. You can use the body of the email to Paste what you Copy.
   * Do you have Word or Pages? Open a new blank document in either of these word processing programs.

2. Now, open a website. Let's use mine. In the address bar, type in www.myparentsfirst.com.
   Choose some of the text and highlight it.
   Copy it, either by:

   * Moving your mouse to the menu bar, then Edit > Copy or
   * Using the keyboard shortcut ⌘ + C

3. Now go back to the blank document. Put your cursor where you want what you copied, pasted and either:

   * From the menu bar, click through Edit > Paste or,
   * Use the keyboard shortcut ⌘ + V

Edit View History Bookmarks	
Undo	⌘ Z
Redo	⌘ Z
Cut	⌘ X
Copy	⌘ C
Paste	⌘ V
Delete	
Select All	⌘ A
Auto Fill Form	⌘ A
Find	▶
Spelling & Grammar	▶
Special Characters	⌥⌘ T

Select All

This will highlight the entire webpage. Once it is highlighted you can choose the edit tool you want to work with.

Select All works the same with other programs. Use it to select all of a document you are working on.

Tip:
Pasting website content into other types of documents often isn't straight-forward. Some websites are darn near impossible to copy and paste. Better just to copy the bit you need and leave the rest alone!

AutoFill Form

This is great for filling out your name and address in forms on websites. It's a good idea to check the form for accuracy after you use this tool!

AutoFill finds your information in the Address Book. How to use the Address Book is just a little further along in the book, on page 123.

Safari

Find

This is another great tool. When you slide your mouse down over Find, this little window will open beside it.

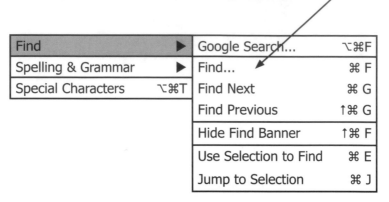

Find	▶	Google Search...	⌥⌘F
Spelling & Grammar	▶	Find...	⌘ F
Special Characters	⌥⌘T	Find Next	⌘ G
		Find Previous	⇧⌘ G
		Hide Find Banner	⇧⌘ F
		Use Selection to Find	⌘ E
		Jump to Selection	⌘ J

Slide your mouse over to Find again, left-click.

A new narrow bar will appear at the top of the webpage you are viewing, below the toolbar.

On the right side of that bar, you will see a spotlight type window where you can type what you are looking for on the webpage.

Try it!

　＊ Go to my website, www.myparentsfirst.com.

　＊ Open *Find*.

　＊ Type "Learning" in the Find window.

　＊ See how it searches the whole page!

Find can be a very handy tool!

Safari

Spelling and Grammar!

Such a great invention! You don't have to worry *too much* about misspelling any more.

Spelling and Grammar scans what you're typing, and points out any words it doesn't recognize. It also lets you know when your grammar is not up to snuff.

Edit View History Bookmarks	
Undo	⌘ Z
Redo	⌘ Z
Cut	⌘ X
Copy	⌘ C
Paste	⌘ V
Delete	
Select All	⌘ A
Auto Fill Form	⌘ A
Find	▶
Spelling & Grammar	▶
Special Characters	⌥⌘ T

As soon as it sees a spelling error, you will see a squiggly red line right under the word. For poor grammar, it shows a green squiggly line This is only to draw your attention to it. It will not automatically correct it; that's still up to you!

Here's an easy way to correct a word:

* Highlight the misspelled word, then right-click!

* A menu of suggestions will open up. This will include the words that your Mac thinks you want to spell, the option to "Learn", as well as a bunch of other choices.

* If you see the correct word on the list, click on it. It will be automatically corrected on your document.

* If you know the word is spelled right, but isn't on the list, click on "Learn" to teach your Mac the new word.

When you click on "Learn" you add the new word to its dictionary!

You're so smart...teaching a computer!

Safari

Special Characters

⇨ ↓ ⇉ ⓘ ♥ ✦ ⚕

These are all samples of special characters. Click around in here to see what's what. If you see a character that you want to put into a document, highlight it! Then click on *Insert*, found on the bottom of the window.

Be your own artist!

86

Safari

View History Bookmarks Wind		
Hide Bookmarks Bar	↑ ⌘	T
Show Status Bar	⌘	/
Show Tab Bar	⌘	T
Hide Toolbar	⌘	I
Customize Toolbar...		
Stop	⌘	.
Reload Page	⌘	R
Make Text Bigger	⌘	+
Make Text Normal Size	⌘	-
Make Text Smaller	⌘	0
View Source	⌥ ⌘	U
Text Encoding		▶

View - Click on the different items under View to see what changes on the Safari window.

When you click on Hide.... it will change to Show...

Click on View Source to see the html coding.

As for Text Encoding, if you read in English, leave it alone. Sites can & do often override this option.

History Bookmarks Window Help			
Back		⌘	[
Forward		⌘	]
Home	↑	⌘	H
Mark Page for SnapBack	⌥	⌘	K
Page SnapBack	⌥	⌘	P
Search Results SnapBack	⌥	⌘	S
Reopen Last Closed Window			
Reopen All Windows From Last Session			
My Parents First			
Google Maps			
Apple			

History - The History menu is pretty straight-forward. I sometimes make use of the list on the bottom of the menu. It shows a list of the last sites you visited.

Safari

Bookmarks!

You don't have to remember the address for every website. Bookmark it, and your computer will remember for you.

Here's how to Bookmark a website:

1. When you find a great website, there are two ways to open the *Add Bookmark* window.

   * Either click on the **"+"** icon on the toolbar, or
   * Click on Bookmarks along the menu bar, then "Add Bookmark".

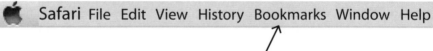

Safari File Edit View History Bookmarks Window Help

2. You can keep the site's name that's already there, or you can change the name to anything you like.

3. Choose the folder you want to file it in.

4. Click on "Add"

Next:
Organizing
bookmarks!

Safari

Click on **Show All Bookmarks** or
the **open-book icon** on the left side of the toolbar,
to open the Bookmarks window!

Bookmarks Window Help		
Show All Bookmarks	⌥ ⌘	B
Add Bookmark...	⌘	D
Add Bookmark for these Tabs...		
Add Bookmark Folder	⌘	N⇧
Bookmarks Bar (99)	▶	

The Safari window will turn into the Bookmark window.

Below the toolbar, you will see the Bookmark Bar.

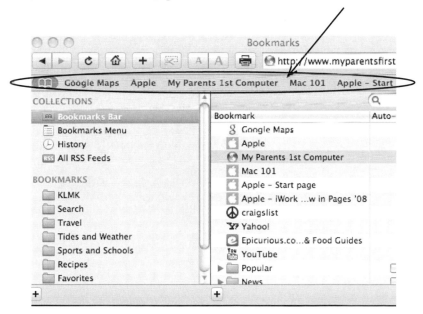

Safari

The sites that show on the Bookmark Bar are filed in the Bookmark Bar folder.

The top few sites in this folder show up along the bar, giving you instant access to them.

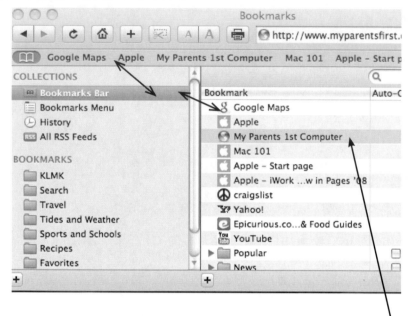

You can rearrange sites in the Bookmarks Bar folder. Here's how!

1. Click over a site to highlight it.

2. Hold your mouse click down and drag the site somewhere else on the list and drop it!

    Try it! See how it changes along the Bookmark Bar.

There's that Drag & Drop again!

You can't rearrange the Collections part of the Bookmark window. **Collections** has folders that Apple has created, and you can't add or change them.

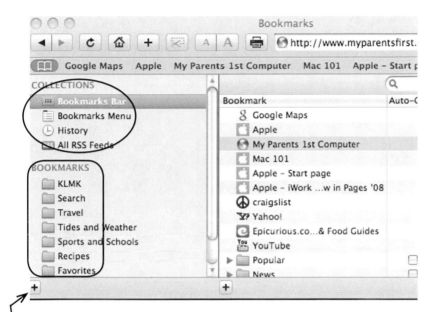

Bookmarks is the place where you can create and name your own Bookmark folders. Here's how:

1. Click on this plus sign!

2. A new "untitled folder" will be instantly created. To name it, just click on "untitled folder" and type a name. Hit the Enter key when you're done.

Now when you *Add a Bookmark,* you can choose where you want to file the address.

You can drag & drop sites from the Bookmark Bar list into folders that you've created!

Safari

Window	Help		
Minimize		⌘	M
Zoom			
Select Next Tab		⌘	}
Select Previous Tab		⌘	{
Move Tab to New Window			
Merge All Windows			
Downloads	⌥	⌘	L
Activity	⌥	⌘	A
Bring All to Front			
Apple			
Google			
My Parents First Computer Guides			

Window
The first six tools under Window are all pretty self explanatory.

If you think these tools will by handy to use, learn their keyboard shortcuts.

It's nice to learn shortcuts for the things you do often!

Click on **Downloads** and a little window will open up with a list of all the files you've recently downloaded. This is the same list found in the *Downloads folder* in *Finder.*

Activity is more for web-tech wizards, not us common folk. So I'm not getting into it! And sorry, for the life of me, I can't figure out what on earth **Bring All to Front** does...

At the bottom of the menu, you will see a list of websites you have open. Click on one to go right there.

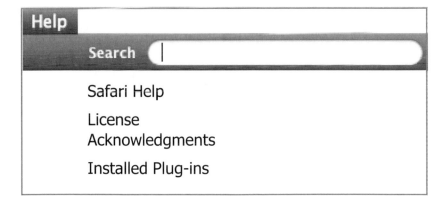

Help works in two ways.

It can help you *find* tools in the menu bar, and it can help you with
how to do something.

Here's how to find
things in the menu bar:

Click on Help, then click your mouse in the Search window and ask away!

Help searches the menu bar for whatever it is you're looking for, and then points it out!

Try it out and you will see what I mean.

Type "form" in the search window and see what happens!

Help

Search (⎮   )

      Safari Help

      License
      Acknowledgments

      Installed Plug-ins

Safari

Here's help with how to do something

Click on "Safari Help", or if that's not there,
  "Show All Results", to open the Mac Help window.

Now that you found it, you'll see that Mac Help is great!
Ask a question, use the Index. You will find good
explanations for whatever you are needing help with.

I find that using the *Index* is better than *Asking a Question*.

Let's try it out!

* Click on Index to open up the alphabet
* Click on "F". See *Forms* on the list?
* Click on "Forms" and see all the how-to-do's!

Searching the Internet

Looking for information on the internet has been made easy with **Search Engines**.

You really don't have to know *how* search engines work to use them. But knowing what they are looking for will make searching easier. You should know what these words mean:

Definitions

Search Engines are dedicated servers with programs that send out *spiders* (also called web crawlers).

Spiders look for *keywords and meta tags* that are imbedded in webpages.

Keywords and Meta Tags are words that describe what's in a website.
You don't see keywords or meta tags when you view a site. They are part of the *HTML* that is hidden, because they are only meant to help search engines find the site.

HTML Hyper Text Markup Language is the computer language that most websites are written in.

Searching the Internet

There are many *search engines*.

Some of the most popular and larger search engines are:

Google, Yahoo, Ask and Mamma

Safari is teamed up with the search engine Google.

Have a look on the right side of the Safari Toolbar and you will see a Google search window right there! This window is a direct link to Google.

Type what you are looking for in the search window!

There is a knack to finding what you are looking for.
Do the practice on the next page
and you'll get the hang of it!

Searching the Internet

Let's do a Google search.

Here's how:

1. Open Safari and click your mouse in the Google search box.

   Or, type in www.google.com in the address bar. On Google's home page you will see a boxed-in window where you can type in your query.

2. Type in the word ***vacation***, then click on Search.

3. A ton of results will show up. It could be thousands. To narrow down your search, be more specific. Maybe you want to holiday in Nova Scotia.

4. Click back into the search box and type: ***vacation Nova Scotia***

5. Search engine *spiders* try to match up your words with website *keywords*. They then will show you all the results they found. You can even be more specific! Maybe you are searching for a bed & breakfast?

6. Click back into the search box and type: ***vacation Nova Scotia Bed & Breakfast***

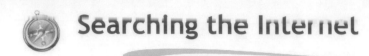

Searching the Internet

When is comes to searching the internet, using better *keywords* means getting better results.

A REALLY GOOD TIP!

If you want a search engine to search for the phrase instead of each individual word,

use "parentheses"!

For example, if you type in Nova Scotia, you will get hits for the single word Nova too. That's okay, if you're looking for a great PBS program!

With parentheses around "Nova Scotia", search engine spiders will only look for the words together.

Mail

Jokes fly around the world via email.
Some are even worse than this one...

Tech Support: What does the screen say now?
Person: It says "hit ENTER when ready".
Tech Support: Well?
Person: How do I know when it's ready?

Mail

Mail

Email is definitely not snail mail! It is almost instantaneous! Practically anything you can create digitally you can email. *Almost!*

You can email:

* personal notes to friends
* digital pictures
* documents
* movies and video clips
* songs...*the list goes on!*

Before we go on, let's talk about an email address.

There are three parts to an email address

1. The name.

2. The "@" sign;
   found above the number 2 on your keyboard, use the shift key to get to it.

3. The server or domain name of where it is sent to.

A typical e-mail address might look like this:

yourname@yourserver.com

There are never, ever, spaces. If it looks like there is a space, there is probably an underscore _ between words.

Mail

Setting up

The first time you open Mail, it will walk you through setting it up. It's not hard to do, but it will make more sense if you have some idea what they are talking about.

Here's the type of information
you are going to need from your ISP.

* Your server's **hostname**, such as mail.nameofyourserver.com

* Your name, **password** and **email address**; for example, you@me.com

* If you are using dial-up, your server's phone number

* **POP** or **IMAP** and **SMTP protocols** (don't you love acronyms!)

* Your **Server's account type**

Notes!_____

_____

_____

_____

D e f i n i t i o n s

SMTP

*S*imple *M*ail *T*ransfer *P*rotocol is the protocol used for
sending email.

POP, IMAP and .ME

*P*ost *O*ffice *P*rotocol and *I*nternet *M*essage *A*ccess *P*rotocol
are both protocols for retrieving email messages. Your server
will use one protocol or the other.

.me is Apple's web service.

Where you are asked for server information, your answers
for incoming and outgoing mail might look like this:

Outgoing mail
- smtp.nameofyourserver.com

Incoming mail
- pop.nameofyourserver.com
  or
- imap.nameofyourserver.com

You are telling your computer what type of protocol your
server prefers.
For retrieving email POP is the most common, IMAP is a
newer version that is a little faster.

Mail

It's nice to have things look and act the way you want them to, so let me show you one more thing before we get into sending and receiving emails.

Setting up your Preferences!

Along Mail's menu bar,
    click Mail, then Preferences.

A window with all these options will open up. Click on each of these headings and see what's in there...

* Select how often you want to check for new mail.

* Set what sound happens when new mail arrives.

* See your email account info & set how they *behave*.

* Tell it how you want junk mail treated.

* Set the size and type of font for your mail. *Font* is the style of printing.

* Set how the spell checker acts.

* Create a "signature" if you like. A signature can be automatically put at the end of your emails. Lots of people use a quote for a signature, often a business will put its name and address.

Bright Ideas

* _____

* _____

* _____

* _____

* _____

* _____

* _____

* _____

*

*

*

*

*

*

Mail

Mail layout

Sidebar — Toolbar

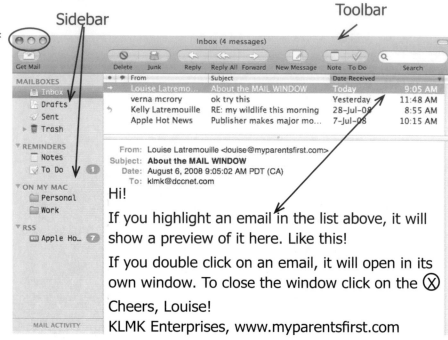

Inbox (4 messages)

Get Mail Delete Junk Reply Reply All Forward New Message Note To Do Search

MAILBOXES
- Inbox
- Drafts
- Sent
- Trash

REMINDERS
- Notes
- To Do (1)

ON MY MAC
- Personal
- Work

RSS
- Apple Ho... (7)

MAIL ACTIVITY

From	Subject	Date Received
Louise Latremo...	About the MAIL WINDOW	Today	9:05 AM
verna mcrory	ok try this	Yesterday	11:48 AM
Kelly Latremouille	RE: my wildlife this morning	28-Jul-08	8:55 AM
Apple Hot News	Publisher makes major mo...	7-Jul-08	10:15 AM

From: Louise Latremouille <louise@myparentsfirst.com>
Subject: **About the MAIL WINDOW**
Date: August 6, 2008 9:05:02 AM PDT (CA)
To: klmk@dccnet.com

Hi!

If you highlight an email in the list above, it will show a preview of it here. Like this!

If you double click on an email, it will open in its own window. To close the window click on the ⊗

Cheers, Louise!

KLMK Enterprises, www.myparentsfirst.com

Highlight a folder in the sidebar to see its contents in the main window. Here, I've got the Inbox highlighted.

See the 1 and the 7 in the sidebar? Those are telling me that I have 1 item that needs attention in the *To Do* folder, and that I have 7 new emails from *Apple Hot News*.

> *   Remember, clicking on the red ⊗ only
>   closes the window, not the program.
>   To quit Mail use these keys: ⌘ + Q

Mail

What's what, on the Mail Toolbar!

Get Mail gets your mail! You can set up how often you want Mail to check for messages automatically, but if you don't like that setting, you can always use this tool instead.

To **delete** an email, highlight it on the list and click on Delete. It will be moved to your Trash can.
Don't worry if you delete something by mistake, it's easy to **get it back from the Trash!**

Here's how to retrieve trash:

1. Click on the Trash folder found in the sidebar to see what's in your Trash.
2. Click on the Message you deleted to highlight it. Now drag & drop it back into the Inbox, or whatever folder you want it in. *There's that drag and drop again!*

It's a good idea to empty all the trash regularly. Here's how:

1. Right-click over Trash in the sidebar, to open the mouse menu.
2. Left click over *Erase Deleted Messages*.

If you only want to delete one message from the trash, highlight it and press delete on your keyboard. Once mail's deleted from the Trash, it's gone, gone, gone.

Mail

Inbox (11 messages)

Get Mail   Delete   Junk   Reply   Reply All   Forward   New Message   Note   To Do   Search

Junk

Junk! Spam! Grrrrr!

Junk mail won't be a problem... *once* you have your Junk Mail filters set!

To find the Junk mail filters in the Menu Bar, *click:*
Mail > Preferences > Junk Mail

If you need help setting your preferences here, be sure to click on the ⑦ in the preferences window for help.

If mail comes to your Inbox that's Junk:
Highlight it, and click on Junk in the toolbar.
All future emails from that sender
will go directly to the Junk mailbox.

If mail is incorrectly marked as Junk mail:
Highlight it and then along the menu bar click:
Message > Mark > Not Junk Mail.

Click on **New Message** to compose a new email. A new message window will open, ready to go! We'll talk more about creating mail in a minute.

Reply
Highlight a message and click on "Reply" to create a new message that is already addressed to the person who sent it to you.
The new message will also, "Re:" the subject line and include a copy of the original message.

You can change what's included in a Reply.
Look along the menu bar and click:
Mail > Preferences > Composing. *Look under Responding.*

If you received mail that was sent to a bunch of people, **Reply All** will send your reply to EVERYBODY.

Click on **Forward** to send Mail you've received on to someone else.

Tip!

Think before you use Forward....

Your JOKES just might be someone else's JUNK!

Mail

These two tools are very similar, but have an important difference. Mainly that, *To Do works with iCal.*

Let's practice!

About Notes

1. Click on Note, to create one.
2. Type: "I'm Learning About Notes."
3. Click on Done.

Click on Notes, in the Sidebar.
Any Notes you write will land in this file.

*To keep the Note front and center,
copy it to your Inbox!*

To show a copy of a note in your Inbox:

1. Highlight the Note in the list,
2. Drag and drop it in the Inbox along the sidebar.

Drag & Drop! I love it!

3. Click on the Inbox and see how your Note is written right there.

Notes can be a very handy tool!

How *To Do!*

1. Click on Notes (in the sidebar) and open your Note.
2. In the note you wrote, highlight *About Notes*.
3. Right-click to open a mouse menu, and choose *New To Do*

   * About Notes will be highlighted and you'll see a circle with an arrow in it.
   * Click on that circle to open some options.

To Do's work together with iCal, your calendar!

You can set the Due Date, a Priority if you want, and which calendar you want this *To Do* to show up on.

If you use iCal a lot, this is a GREAT thing!

Open iCal

To see the To Do's, click on the thumbtack that's on the bottom right side of the window.

You can even drag & drop To Do's directly onto the Calendar. Try it out! It's sure a great way to stay organized.

> Use *To Do* directly with received email.
> Say you got emailed a scheduled appointment. Just highlight part of the mail and create a New To Do!
> FANTASTIC.

Mail

Writing a New Message

Click on "New Message" along the Mail toolbar to create a new email.

New Message

A new mail window will open. You'll see spaces for you to fill in the recipient's address, the subject of the message and a blank space for you to write your message.

The New Message window has its own toolbar for mail!

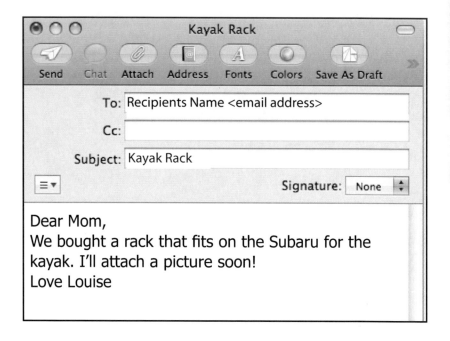

< >
Parentheses always surround an email address.

Mail

Sending email

When you have finished writing your mail, simply click on Send, found in the toolbar.

Attachments

You can attach any type of file to an email message. But before sending an attachment, you should be aware of a couple of things:

* The size of the file attached. Pictures can be large files and how fast they can be sent or received depends on your - and the recipient's, internet speed. Sending a large file to someone who uses dial-up can really bung things up!

* Servers often set size restrictions too. For instance, a movie might be too large a file to send.

* Corporate servers often pre-screen all attachments, so your attachment might not get through at all.

* Does the receiver have the right program to open the file? It's very frustrating getting an attachment that your computer can't figure out how to open!

Let's practice!

Mail

Here are two ways to attach a file.

Drag & Drop or using Attach in the toolbar.

If you can get to the file you are attaching from your desktop, Drag & Drop is the way to go. Let's attach a file from the Documents folder to an email and send it to yourself to practice. *Yes, you can email yourself!*

Here's how to Drag & Drop a file:

1. Start a new message. Type your email address in the *To* space and give it a subject, maybe, "Drag and Drop"!

2. Click on the Documents folder along the Dock to view its contents. *(I hope there is something in there!)*

3. Click on your choice of a file to attach.

4. **Drag and drop** the file over to the body of your email, *where you would write something.* If you attach a picture, you will see the picture on the email. If you attach a document, you will see an icon with the file's name on your email.

5. Click on Send! Voilà!

If it's not already back to you, click on Get Mail.

We'll open this email in a minute and go over what's what. But first, let's go over how to attach a file using the toolbar.

Here's how to attach, with Attach!

Click on the paperclip icon along the toolbar.

When you click on *Attach*, you'll open a window that is similar to the Finder window. You'll be able to find any file in your computer.

The best part of using Attach is the Search window! Type the file's name, or even just part of the name, in the Search window. A list of what you might be looking for will appear. *It's a very good thing!*

If you're not using the Search window, then you'll need to know the best place to look. **Look under PLACES!**

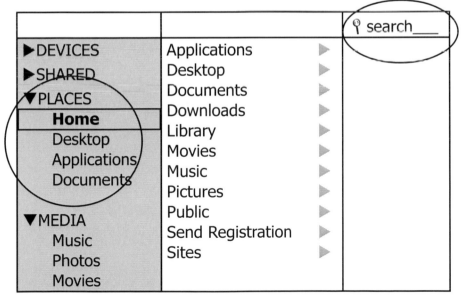

Attachments: Find window

See where I've circled "Home". *This is the **Home Folder.**
It's not actually named Home*. *Yours will be named whatever
your user account name is.* **But you will know it's your
Home Folder by the little house icon beside it!**

The Home folder stores all *YOUR* personal information.
It's where you go to find *your* stuff.

	Pictures ↕	⚲ search ___
►DEVICES	Applications ▶	iPhoto Library ▶
►SHARED	Desktop ▷	**Photo Booth ▶** ——
▼PLACES	Documents ▷	
🏠 **Home**	Downloads ▷	
Desktop	Library ▷	
Applications	Movies ▷	
Documents	Music ▷	
	Pictures ▶	
▼MEDIA	Public ▷	
Music	Sites ▷	
Photos	▷	
Movies		

Click over your Home folder, and you will see its contents in
the next column.

Keep clicking on folders: eventually you will find your file!

Here, I clicked on Places, then:

Home > Pictures > Photo Booth > Photo1.jpg

> ▶ If you see an arrow like this, click on it to see where it leads!

> This space reflects the name of the folder you are looking in.

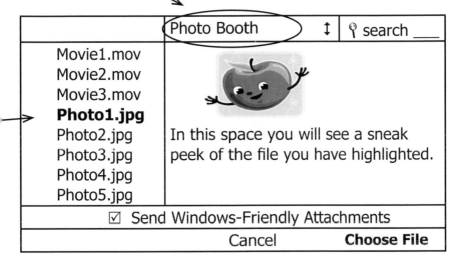

Photo Booth ⇕	⚲ search ___
Movie1.mov	
Movie2.mov	
Movie3.mov	
Photo1.jpg	
Photo2.jpg	In this space you will see a sneak
Photo3.jpg	peek of the file you have highlighted.
Photo4.jpg	
Photo5.jpg	
☑ Send Windows-Friendly Attachments	
Cancel	**Choose File**

Click on Cancel if you decide you don't want to attach anything after all.

Click on Choose File to be returned to your email with the file attached!

> **TIP**: Make sure there is a tick ☑ in the *Send Windows-Friendly* box!

Mail

Opening and Sorting Mail

Headers

Between Mail's toolbar and the list of all your emails you'll see a skinny row of headers; From, Subject, Date.

These headers can help you organize your mail. Here's how:

Left click on any of the headers and your email will re-organize itself according to that header.

For instance, if I'm looking for another email that my Mom sent, I would highlight an email from her, then click on "From" in the the headers.

All the emails are now sorted by who sent them, with Mom's emails front and center! Click on the other headers and see how the emails can be shuffled around. Click on the header again and the sort order is reversed. A - Z becomes Z - A!

You will often see these symbols to the left of your emails. **What do they mean?**

↺   This means you have replied to that email.

→   This means you have forwarded that email.

●   This means it is unopened mail.

Mail

Right-click along the header line and see other headers that you can have. It's easy to change.

●	From	Subject	Date
→	Apple Hot News	Quick Tip	Today
	Mom	Re: Kayak Rack	Yesterday
↺	Danny	Mrs Kyles choc cake	Sept 9, 2008

From: Mom <mom@yahoo.com>
Subject: Kayak Rack
Date: Sept 8, 2008
To: Louise < louise@myparentsfirst.com>
📎 1 Attachment, 75 KB   Save   Quick Look

Hi Louise,
Now you can go anywhere with your kayak!
Love Mom

Highlight an email to see it in this preview pane!

To open an email on a full screen, double click on it. *You don't see the toolbar when you view an email full-screen.*

Moving Mail
Drag & Drop! If you have created your own special mailboxes in the sidebar, such as Personal or Work, you can easily move mail to them.
Just highlight the email, then Drag & Drop it into the mailbox you want it in!

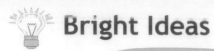

Bright Ideas

✳ _____

✳ _____

✳ _____

✳ _____

✳ _____

✳ _____

✳ _____

✳ _____

✳

✳

✳

✳

✳

✳

The Apple Cart

You'll love the goodies
in this Apple Cart.
Gobble up the simple steps and you'll
be using them in no time!

The Apple Cart

Address Book

The Address Book!

The Address book is the best example of how much Mac applications love to cooperate with each other.

Of course it works with Mail, and Mail cooperates with other programs when you want to email something, such as a picture from iPhoto! It can also work with iCal to help you keep track of important dates.

Click on the Address Book icon along the Dock to open it.

Remember, you can always go through Finder to find any application. Here's how to find the Address Book:

Finder > Places > Applications > Address Book

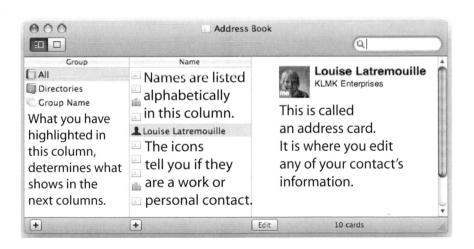

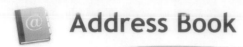

Address Book

The first column in the Address Book window has these folders:

All, for all your contacts.

Directories, if your computer is part of an office network that has a directory service, this could access their directory!

Group Name, for creating your own personal distribution lists! It's very easy to do once you have added contacts! First click on **+** to add a new group. Name it. Then go back up and highlight *All* to show your contacts in the 2nd column. Drag names from the 2nd column into your new group. A copy of the address goes into the Group!

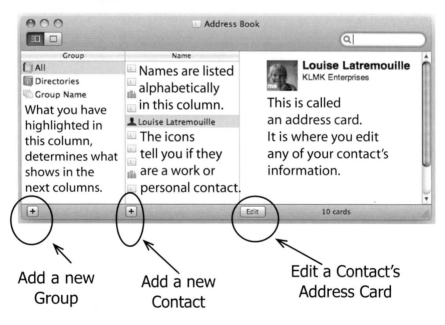

Add a new
Group

Add a new
Contact

Edit a Contact's
Address Card

Don't worry about adding a group or contact by mistake.
To delete an entry:
* Click your mouse over the entry you don't want, to highlight it, and hit Delete on your keyboard.

Address Book

Let's add YOU, to the Address Book!

To Add a contact:

1. Highlight "**All**" in the first column.

2. Click on the add sign, **+**, that's **under the 2nd** column.

3. "No Name" will show up in 2nd column and a blank Address Card will show up in the 3rd.

4. **Click your mouse in the 3rd column**, in the space labeled "First". Type in your first name.

5. Use the Tab key on your keyboard to **Tab** through the address card and fill out the rest of your information!

You can change how the address cards look.

Under Address Book along the menu bar > Preferences

Address Book > Preferences

In the window that opens, click on General & Template.

Under General, set how you want the cards sorted, set the address format to the right country, and the size of the font you want to see on the cards.

Under Template, click on the plus or minus signs to add or delete fields. Click on the tiny up/down arrows between "**home ♦** Phone" to change the field. ie: *home* to *work*. ⬈

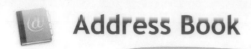

Address Book

Adding email addresses to your Address Book

The best and easiest way to add an email address
to your address book is to
grab the address from an email sent to you!

●	From	Subject	Date
→	Apple Hot News	Quick Tip	Today
	Mom	Re: Kayak Rack	Yesterday
↺	Danny	Mrs Kyles choc cake	Sept 9, 2008

From: Mom <mom@momsserver.net>
Subject: Kayak Rack
   Date: Sept 8, 2008
      To: Louise < louise@myparentsfirst.com>
📎 Attachment, 75 KB   Save   Quick Look

Here's how:
1. View the email your friend sent you.
2. Move your mouse over their name, *beside From:*
3. Right click to open the mouse menu
4. Choose, "Add to Address Book"

That's it!

When you start a new email message you can click on the
Address Book to insert your friend's address!

Mail will also remember
addresses. If you start typing
your friend's address in the
"To:" box, it will fill in the rest!

126

iCal

iCal is a great tool to help you stay organized.

View by Day, Week or Month
Scroll forward or back in time using the arrows

Create new calendars for home, work or school by clicking on the (+) Add button. Events are color coded to each calendar.

To add appointments: Choose a calendar (for color coding), then right-click over a day to open the option, "New Event". Voilà!   Now you can type in the date square!

To add events from Mail to iCal: When both the iCal and Mail windows are open, highlight some text on an email, then drag & drop it on a date in iCal. *It can't get any simpler than that!*

Birthdays! If you have entered birthdays in the Address Book, iCal will post them for you! To show birthdays, along the menu bar click; iCal > Preferences. Enable Birthdays.

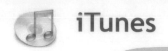

iTunes

Let the music roll!

iTunes is Apple's music application. You'll not find an easier music program than iTunes. On the next few pages I'll show you what's what.

Here's the layout.

Rewind
Forward
Pause/Play

Volume

Shows
what's playing

Change how
your window
looks with **View.**
I'm showing the
list view here.

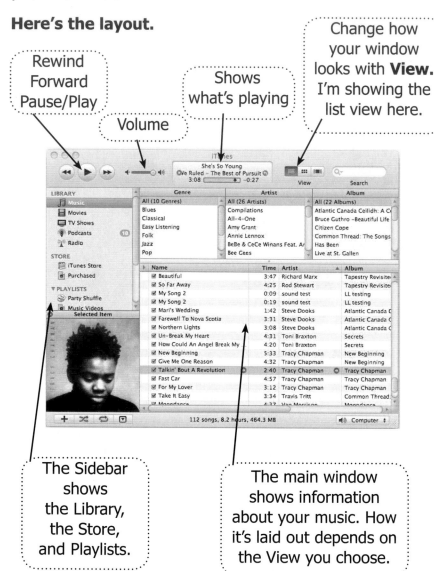

The Sidebar
shows
the Library,
the Store,
and Playlists.

The main window
shows information
about your music. How
it's laid out depends on
the View you choose.

128

iTunes

Here's how to view your music:

1. Click on a folder in the **sidebar** to see what's in it.
2. Find the **View** buttons on the toolbar.
3. Play with the View buttons to see the different layouts that iTunes has!

Album Cover view

List view

Cover Flow view. *Very cool!*

I show the List view on the previous page. You can sort and see what music you have in your library by Genre, Artist or Album. Click around on different headings and different views to see how things get rearranged.

Here's how to Play your music!

1. Choose a folder in the sidebar, to see your music in the main window. You can play the whole folder or highlight a single song to play it.
2. Click on the Play arrow on the top left corner of the window. A little speaker icon will show beside the song that's playing.

   The Play button turns into to Pause when music is playing. To stop playing a song, click on it!

Here are some great tools!

On the bottom left corner of the window you will see these four tools. Add a Playlist — straight-forward. Use Shuffle and Repeat when you are playing songs, they turn blue when they're active. Show Artwork in the sidebar, or not.

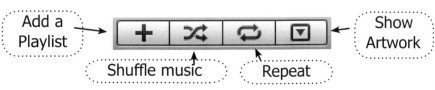

Add a Playlist

Shuffle music

Repeat

Show Artwork

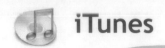

iTunes

The Sidebar: Library

Music is downloaded into the music folder when you purchase it from the iTunes Store or import it from your own CD.

Movies and TV Shows are filed here, once purchased from the iTunes Store.

Podcasts can be subscribed to from the iTunes Store. Many podcasts are free.

Podcasts are pretty cool. For an example, you can download a free subscription to the CBS Evening News.

Once you have downloaded the subscription, you can view the news on-line. Every night, it will be automatically updated. Automatic & frequent updates is the key to podcasts. Whenever a new *feed* is available, your podcast subscription is updated.

LIBRARY
>   Music
>   Movies
>   TV Shows
>   Podcasts
>   Radio

STORE
>   iTunes Store
>   Purchased

DEVICES
>   Morgan's Ipod

PLAYLISTS
>   Party Shuffle
>   Music Videos
>   Recently Added
>   Recently Played
>   Top 25 Most Played
>   untitled playlist

Radio. WOW! You can listen to radio stations that broadcast digitally, from all over the world!

130

The Sidebar: Store

The iTunes Store has a variety of things for sale that can be downloaded into your computer. Music, Movies, TV Shows, Audiobooks... All in digital form.

To purchase or download items from the store, you first have to create an iTunes account. If you already have an AOL or Apple account you can use those.

It's very simple to create an iTunes account. Along the menu bar, click through; Store > Create New Account.

You'll be asked for your name and address. If you want to purchase anything you will have to give a credit card number.

When you download a purchase, you will see a copy of it in the Purchased folder and in its genre's folder; ie, music in the Music folder, podcasts in the Podcasts folder.

If iTunes quits, or your computer gets shut down before a purchase has finished downloading, the download should resume the next time you open iTunes.

*If it doesn't, click
Store > Check for Purchases.*

*ALL SALES ARE FINAL!
Your account is charged when you buy!*

131

iTunes

The Sidebar: Devices

If you attach an iPod to your Mac, Devices will show up. If no device is connected, you won't even see Devices in the sidebar!

If you have an iPod, you'll use iTunes to manage the music in it. More about iPods next!

DEVICES
  Morgan's Ipod
PLAYLISTS
  Party Shuffle
  Music Videos
  Recently Added
  Recently Played
  Top 25 Most Played
  untitled playlist

Playlists

A Playlist is a group of songs that you put together! iTunes has created a few playlists for you to start with. You can delete these or add new ones!

Here's how to make a Playlist:

1. Click on the add sign (**+**) on the bottom left corner of the iTunes window. You will create a new folder under Playlists, named "untitled playlist".

2. Click over untitled playlist and give it a new name, maybe Dinner Party.

3. Click your mouse back into the Library > Music.

4. In the main window, click on a song to choose it.

5. Drag & drop the song into your new playlist!

When you put a song in a playlist, it will still be in your Library. You are not moving the music files, you are creating links to the songs in your library.
When you delete a playlist, you are only deleting the playlist. *The songs will still be in your Library.*

iPod & iTunes

Remember when...

The iPod

An iPod is an mp3 player. It's today's hottest way to listen to your favorite music, and it's no wonder why. These little devices give you terrific sound and hold hundreds, — thousands — of songs.

iPods don't have any moving parts, so they don't skip like a portable CD player does!

On the next few pages we'll learn some of the basics on how to use an iPod. And, learn how they work with iTunes.

Boy oh boy, we've come a long way...

iPod Basics

iPods work with your Mac and iTunes. They play music downloaded from iTunes. iPod batteries are charged when you connect it to your Mac. And with Apple, your iPod will always have the latest updates too!

What's what on an iPod?

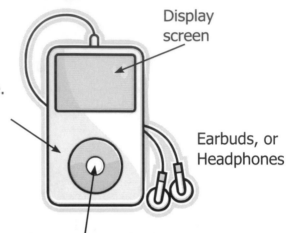

Display screen

The Menu Wheel. Works like a mouse. Drag your finger around it and the highlighted line on the screen moves up, down, left or right.

Earbuds, or Headphones

The Select Button, in the centre of the Menu Wheel. Once you have what you want highlighted, click on this button to select it.

There is a "hold" button on an iPod. Use this to make sure you don't accidentally turn it on or off, or to hold the volume from changing. Like many things on an iPod, it's a versatile tool!

On the bottom of an mp3 player, you will see a connection port.

Different models might also have an on/off switch.

Connection Cable

One end of the cable connects to your mp3 player and the other, to a USB port on your computer. Plug the USB end in first to your Mac, then connect the other end to your iPod.

With some models, you have to squeeze both sides of the connector to release it from the iPod.

Took me a frustrated while to figure that one out... yanking on the cord... sheezzze!

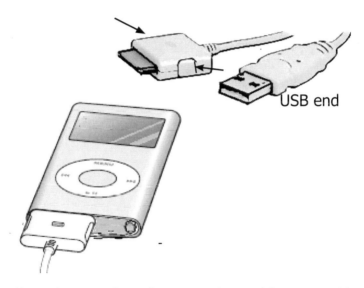

USB end

iPod's recharge when they are plugged into your Mac.

Tip.... *The computer has to be turned on to recharge!*

Sync ... synchronize

"Sync" is a term you'll see often.
It simply means your iPod and iTunes
are working together.

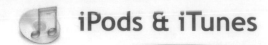

iPods & iTunes

Putting Music into iTunes from a CD

Let's Practice!

1.   Click on iTunes along the dock to open it up.

2.   Insert a CD into the CD slot on your Mac. Two things will happen:

   *   You will see a temporary icon representing the CD show up on your desktop and,

   *   iTunes will ask you if you would like to import the music from the CD.

      *   **Say Yes**, if you want to import ALL the songs from the CD.

      *   **Say No,** if you want to choose which songs to import.

   For our practice, click on NO.

3.   On the sidebar, you will see the title of the CD under Devices.

   If you are connected to the internet you will see the title. If you are not connected, it will just say untitled CD.

4.   In the main window you will see a list of all the songs, along with a ✓ mark in boxes beside them.

   If you are connected to the internet you will see the song titles. If you are not connected, the songs will be listed as tracks.

5. Songs with a check mark beside it will be copied into iTunes. If you don't want a song, click over the mark to un-tick it.

6. Once you have only the songs you want ticked, click on "Import CD" at the bottom of the window. Only the songs that are ticked will be imported.

* You'll see a little bullet beside each song as it downloads, and a green checked circle once the download is complete!

Click on the eject icon at the bottom right corner to eject your CD.

Check out your new music in your Music Library!

Double-click on a title to play the song!

Rewind, Play & Fast fwd
Click on Play ▶
and it will change to **II** ,
which means stop or pause.
◀◀ means rewind & this means go forward ▶▶

iPods & iTunes

Putting Music on your iPod

1. Connect your iPod to your Mac with the connection cable that came with the iPod. Plug the USB end in first, then the other end to the iPod. If it's not already there, iTunes will open.

    ＊ You will see your iPod show up under Devices along the sidebar of iTunes.

2. iTunes will want to sync with your iPod.

    You have a choice here to let it sync, or to add music manually.

    ＊ Let it **sync** with your iTunes and your iPod will be updated to match everything in your iTunes. If you are connecting to someone else's iTunes, don't sync!

    ＊ Choose to **manually manage** the music and you can pick and choose what songs you would like to add to your iPod from iTunes.

    To manually add music from iTunes to your iPod...

Drag and Drop!

Yep, it's that simple. Open your Music Library. Click over the song you want. Drag & Drop the song into your iPod along the sidebar!

Click on the eject icon and disconnect your iPod!

Go for a nice walk and enjoy your music!

138

Why having internet access is important

iTunes, and other music programs, are made to work with the internet. Besides having access to the iTunes Store and a great selection of music, videos, audio-books and more, being on the internet makes organizing your music much easier.

When you put a CD into your Mac, iTunes reads it. Then, iTunes goes to the web to find information about the CD, the artists and song titles.

You can import CD's to your Mac without the internet, but each song (or "track") will be titled something like track 01, track 02, track 03, etc.

It's a lot of work adding song titles manually. It's not hard to do, just time consuming. All you have to do is click your mouse over the track you want to name. The space will change into a box you can type in.

When you connect your iPod to your Mac, it will want to sync with iTunes! If you choose to sync, the titles that you have in iTunes are what will show up on your iPod.

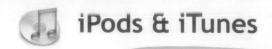

iPods & iTunes

Here's a little about audio (music) files.

Stuff you don't need to know, but knowing it can make things easier to understand!

Mp3 is an acronym for a type of audio file. It stands for Moving Picture Experts Group Audio Layer 3. *There, now you know more than most!!*

Though mp3 files are the most popular, they are not the only kind of audio file around. Here are just a few others, and what the acronyms stand for.

.wma	-	Windows Media Audio
.wav	-	Waveform Audio
.aac	-	Advanced Audio Coding
.asf	-	Advanced Streaming Format
.vqf	-	Vector Quantization Format

and then, there is MP4!

Mp4 was designed with sending videos in mind. It is quietly becoming the standard for sending all sorts of media!

Mp4 players are generally larger than mp3 players.

What is so great about mp4 technology is that it is designed to work with and support other formats! It is also designed to grow, update and adapt to whatever is coming its way. It's pretty cool technology!

iPods & iTunes

iPods play mp3 files. When you copy music from a CD, iTunes turns the song into an mp3 file. Music downloaded from the internet is already in mp3 form.

Mp3 files are a type of audio file that is very compact. So, putting lots of mp3 files on your Mac won't take up a ton of space on your hard drive.

Tip!
When you plug your ipod
into another computer,

DON'T SYNC IT TO THEIR iTUNES!

or you will lose your music and gain theirs!

Use the option to "manually manage"
the music instead.

Remember, Sync means Synchronize!

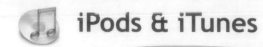

iPods & iTunes

Every music program has these tools:
a **Ripper** and an **Encoder**

> In iTunes,
> you won't see the term "Ripper"
> Ripping is simply called Importing.

Importing

Ripping. The word sounds a little scary, but that's the term the music industry has used for years when copying music. You "rip" files from a CD **to copy the music** onto the hard drive in your computer.

Don't worry. You don't erase or affect the CD in any way, shape or form when you *rip* - or import music from it.

An Encoder

Converts the music you are copying into mp3 files.

The music on CD's is in a file format that is huge!
The Encoder converts and compresses the songs into tiny mp3 files. *Very clever thing, this encoder!*

iPods & iTunes

Disconnecting your iPod

It is very important that you tell iTunes that you are going to disconnect your iPod.

Don't disconnect from your computer until your mp3 player says it's OK to disconnect, or you might damage its memory.

Here are a few ways to disconnect:

* Click the eject icon at the bottom of the iTunes window
* From the menu bar, click through Controls > Eject
* With your keyboard, click Control > Eject

Need to write down some notes?

_____

_____

_____

_____

_____

_____

_____

_____

_____

_____

_____

_____

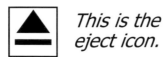

This is the eject icon.

Bright Ideas

*

*

*

*

*

*

*

*

*

*

*

*

*

*

iPhoto - you'll get the hang of it in a snap!

Click on the iPhoto icon along the dock to open it up and let's have a look around!

The sidebar has folders that help you organize your photos. The icons along the bottom are for the most common tasks.

But, first things first....
Importing pictures from your camera!

Digital cameras work with iPhoto. Simply connect your camera to your Mac with a USB cord and your pictures will start to download.

Your digital camera should come with a USB cord. One end is specific to a transfer port on your camera, the other end fits into a USB port on your Mac. If you don't have a USB cord, bring your camera with you when you go out to buy one, so you get the right size.

iPhoto

Transferring Photos from a Camera

1. **Connect your camera to your computer using the USB cable.** The port on your camera probably has a cover on it!

> Your pictures should load immediately, but if they don't...
>
> Different cameras will have different preferences when it comes to exporting pictures. If the iPhoto import option does not open right after you connect your camera to your Mac, look for these things:
>
> * Check that the USB cable is connected firmly at both ends.
> * Check that your camera is turned on.
> * Check what *mode* your camera is in:
>   * Some cameras like to be in regular picture taking mode,
>   * Some like to be set to the viewing mode,
>   * Still others might have a special setting for exporting!

2. Once downloaded, a window will open where you can **give your photos an event name,** or you can name them later. If you leave the field blank, iPhoto will name the event(s) by the dates.

3. You can describe the event in the description field.

4. You can **import all the photos, or you can select which ones you want** by clicking over a photo and choosing "Import Selected" at the bottom of the window.

iPhoto

There are two great options at the bottom of the window, **Autosplit and Hide**:

"Autosplit events after importing"
Tick Autosplit, and your photos will be sorted into events by the dates the pictures were taken.

"Hide photos already imported"
If there are pictures in your camera that you have previously imported, you can hide them from the import view, by ticking Hide.

5. **To import all of the photos from your camera, click on "Import All".**

   Just before the import is finished, iPhoto will ask **if you want to delete the originals** from your camera and, if there are duplicate pictures, if you want to import them too.

   ∗ **Say Yes** to Delete the originals and you will clear the memory in your camera, freeing up space in your camera again!

   ∗ **Say No,** if you want to keep the originals in your camera.

That's it! Well almost. **Here's how to disconnect!**
Drag the camera's icon from Devices in the sidebar, to the Trash - this *ejects* it. Then turn off your camera and disconnect the USB cable.

Important! Do not disconnect your camera until the photo transfer is finished!

iPhoto

LIBRARY
Events
Photos

RECENT
Summer Holidays
Last 12 Months
Last Import
Flagged
Trash

ALBUMS
Summer Times
Squash Tournys

SLIDESHOWS
Last Import Slides...
Holiday Slideshow...

**The Sidebar,
is your source list.**
It is where you can find and
organize your photos.

**The Library
Events and Photos** is where
your photos will land when you
download them.

**Click on Events to see one
thumbnail image from each
event you have.**

**Click on Photos to see ALL the
photos in ALL Events.**

To see the pictures from only one
event, double-click over a single
event thumbnail.
If you only see one picture in
the event, check your preferences. On the menu bar, click;
iPhoto > Preferences > Events.

* You can re-name an event simply by clicking over its title.

* You can sort events via the menu bar, View > Sort
Events. Then choose how you want them sorted.

* You can scroll through pictures when looking at events,
simply by moving your mouse over the Event's thumbnail.

* You can change the cover photo on an event. Scroll
through the pictures. When you see the one you want,
hit the space bar.

148

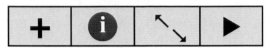

At the bottom left corner of the iPhoto window, you will see these buttons.

 Click on the **ADD** sign, and you will open a small window that gives you options **to create**:

A New Album, a Smart Album or a Slideshow.
More on Albums and Slideshows on the next page!

&

You can also create and then order from Apple
Cards, Calendars and even a Book created from
your pictures. Click into these options to check
them out. Apple makes them easy to use, and if you
decide to buy something, they are very well priced!

&

If you have an Apple *Mobile Me* account, you will
be able to publish your photos to your own on-line
gallery.

 Information! Each photo has its own information.

You can edit this
information by clicking
into the spaces in the right
column. Change the title,
even the date and time the
photo was taken. Give it a
rating and keywords to help
you find it some other time.
Add a description!

Information	
title	the Pup
date	14/09/2008
time	12:30:17
rating	***
keyword	dogs, walks
kind	JPEG Image
size	1600 x 1200
description	

Click on this to view your pictures **Full Screen!** This is a nice way to look at your photos one at a time. You have to have your mouse down at the bottom of the screen to see a toolbar, in full screen mode.

Click on the arrows on the right side of the toolbar to scroll through your pictures.

I think this is the best screen to **compare pictures** in. Click on the picture you think is best, then click on Compare (on the left side of the toolbar). Now you will see two windows. With the picture you like on the left, you can scroll through the pictures on the right to compare your photo prowess!

Click on the ⊗ at the right side of the toolbar, to go back to the regular viewing mode!

Play a Slideshow of an event or album. Click on this to play a slideshow of your pictures. A window will pop up, giving you some options for basic settings and music. Tick what you want, un-tick what you don't!

This will play a slideshow of your event or album; it doesn't save the slideshow. If you want to create a slideshow, click on this Slideshow icon, found on the bottom toolbar. More on slideshows coming up!

iPhoto

Creating Albums
Here's how to create an album!

+ | ⓘ | ↖↘ | ▶

1. Click on the Add sign, then *Album* in the window that pops open. Give it a name. Click OK.

Album | Smart Album | MobileMe | Slideshow | Book | Card | Calendar

2. In the sidebar, you will see a new folder for your album. It will have the name you gave it, or be "untitled album".

3. To add pictures to your album, go back up to your Library. Click on Photos to get individual photos, or Events if you want to add an entire event.

4. Click over a picture you want, then...***drag & drop* it into the new album folder** you just created!

*   You can rearrange pictures in albums, simply by dragging a photo to a new position. This is easiest if you are viewing thumbnails. If you're not, in the menu bar click View > Thumbnails > Show.

*   You can safely delete pictures you don't want in an album. Deleting a picture in an album does not delete the picture in your Library, BUT deleting a picture in the Library deletes it in your album!

*   If you change the information or edit a picture in an album, the changes you make will be made in your Library too.

*   *If you want to include all or most of the photos from an event in an album SELECT the event before you create the folder.*

151

iPhoto

Create a Smart Album

If you add information to your pictures, such as keywords, titles, rating them etc., you can create a Smart Album.

You can add information to both Events *and* individual photos.

Information	
title	Moms Rose
date	14/01/2009
time	4:30:17
rating	*****
keyword	garden
kind	JPEG Image
size	1600 x 1200
description	

Here's how to create a Smart Album

1. Click on the Add sign, and then *Smart Album* in the window that pops open.

2. Adjust the first field showing, to suit the conditions you want; Album, Rating, Description, Title, etc. Then fill in the adjoining fields. You can add more conditions by clicking on the Add **+** sign in this window.

3. *Click "OK" and you're done!* iPhoto will instantly gather all the photos you have that meet the conditions you created.

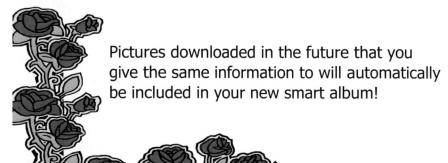

Pictures downloaded in the future that you give the same information to will automatically be included in your new smart album!

152

Creating Slideshows

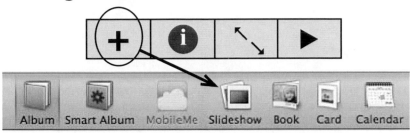

Album   Smart Album   MobileMe   Slideshow   Book   Card   Calendar

Click on the Add sign **+** , then Slideshow to create a
Slideshow you want to save. *Tip: If you want to include all
or most of the photos from an event in a slideshow, SELECT
it first. You can always add or delete photos from a show.*

Here's how to create a Slideshow

1. Click on the Add sign, and then *Slideshow* in the window
   that pops open. Give it a name.

2. Click OK. You will see a new folder for your slideshow, in
   the sidebar.

3. Go back in the sidebar, up to your Library and click on
   Photos.

4. Click over the pictures you want, then **drag & drop
   them** *into the new Slideshow folder* you just created!

   Don't be scared!

Now that you have the pictures in the slideshow, you can
fancy up its presentation! Such as adding music, deciding
how the slides will transition, rearranging the pictures...

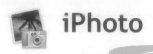

iPhoto

Here's How to Edit your Show!

From the sidebar, click on the slideshow you have created to open it. A window similar to this one will open.

All the pictures in the slideshow, show up along the top pane of the window. **This is where you can rearrange your pictures.** Simply drag & drop them in the order your want!

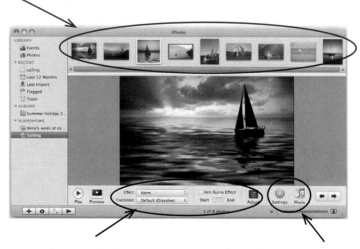

Along the bottom of the window you will see your editing tools. **These editing tools are for setting how your slideshow will be presented.**

The first group of tools are for **editing the effects on a single slide.**

The second group, **Settings and Music, are for setting the effects for the entire show.**

iPhoto

Slideshow Settings

**Open a slideshow and
click on Settings.**

Settings   Music

You will see these options to decide on and set!

* How long each slide plays for.
  ----
* How you want the slides to transition.
* What speed you want the slides to transition.
  ----
* If you want the slideshow to repeat itself.
* If you want the pictures to scale to full screen.
* If you want the Ken Burns effect. (moving)
* If you want the photo titles to show.
* If you want to show how you rated the slide.
* If you want to show the slideshow controls. This is good,
  in case you want to pause the show.
  ----
* If you want the music to repeat itself during the show.
* If you want the slideshow to be only as long as the music
  you select for it!
  ----
* Adjust the Slideshow format if you are playing it on
  another screen, such as a TV.

  Click OK when you think
  you've got it right.

  You can change these
  settings at any time.

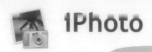

iPhoto

Slideshow Music

Having music playing in the background makes watching a slideshow special. Here's how!

1. First, in the sidebar, make sure the slideshow you want is highlighted and showing in the main window.

2. Click on the Music icon to open your music options.

3. Along the top, make sure there is a tick ✓ in the "Play music during slideshow" box. ***By the way, this is where you would turn off the music option too!***

    The little window that opens is divided into two parts:

    ✻ The top part shows folders that the music you are looking for could be in. There is a Sample Music folder, but you can also use music from iTunes or even Garage Band!

    ✻ The bottom part shows the music that is in the folder you have highlighted in the top part.

    There is also a Search window. If you type in the name of the song or the artist, it will search the folder you have highlighted.

4. Highlight the song you would like to play during the show.

5. Click OK!

Click on the Play ▶ button and enjoy the show. You can re-edit the show as many times as you want.

Want to make some notes?
_____

_____

_____

_____

_____

_____

_____

_____

_____

_____

_____

_____

_____

_____

Don't worry about taking up hard drive space!

When you create albums, slideshows, books, etc., you are not copying your photos into those creations.

You are creating *links* to photos in your Library.

You can create as many albums and slideshows as you like without using up the hard drive!

About Deleting Pictures

When you delete a picture from an album, etc, you are only deleting its link to your library.

BUT... If you delete a picture from your Library, it is gone not only from the Library, but from any Albums or Slideshows it was in!

Deleted Library pictures go to the Trash can.

You can get a photo back from the Trash.
Simply open your trash, then drag & drop the photo back into your Library!
If you empty your trash...
the pictures are unretrievable!

Two great editing tips:
Duplicating and Reverting!

Duplicating.

Remember, when you create albums, slideshows, etc., each photo is "linked" to the original photo in your Library.

When you edit a photo, the edits will show in every album, slideshow, whatever you have that photo in.

If you would like to edit a photo without affecting everywhere it's linked to, duplicate it, then edit the duplicate.

Select the picture you want.
From the menu bar click Photos > Duplicate

Reverting

With the latest version of iPhoto you don't have to worry about really screwing up a picture when you try and edit it. iPhoto always has an original of your photo in its memory.

Select the picture you want.
From the menu bar click,
Photos > Revert to Original

Also, don't forget about Edit > Undo,
if you're just working on a photo.

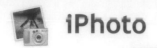
iPhoto

One more tip!
You can re-organize your events and photos!
When your photos are downloaded into your Library, the Events iPhoto created might not be how you would like them. No worries!

You can move photos from one event into another.
Click on Photos to view all your pictures. Click on the picture you want to move. Then simply drag it from one event and drop it into another!

You can merge an event into another!
Click on Events to view all your events. Click on the event you want to move; then, drag it over top of the event you want it merged with — and drop it!

Editing Pictures

You can do basic editing of your pictures with iPhoto. Things like adjusting the brightness of a picture to cropping it. All of the tools are well laid out and easy to use.

Select a picture in your Library, *then click on the Edit icon*, found along the bottom of the window.

The individual photo will open, and you'll see this toolbar.

Learn what's what, next!

Editing

Rotate. Click on this to rotate your photo, 90 degrees at a time.

Crop. Click on this to trim your photo down to size. If you want to be sure of the size or shape of the photo, use the "Constrain" option.

Straighten. Unlike Rotate, this will let you adjust the horizontal aspect of the picture; plus or minus 10 degrees at a time.

Enhance. This will automatically enhance the exposure and brightness of your picture.

Red Eye. What a great thing to be able to fix red-eye! **Here's how:**

1. If it's not a closeup, zoom in on the picture using the Zoom slider - find it on the very bottom right side of the window, in the grey area.

2. Leaving the size setting to Automatic is a good idea.

3. Move your mouse to the center of a pupil, and click.

4. If you like the result, click Done.

5. If you don't like the result, go to the menu bar and click Edit > Undo.

iPhoto

 Retouch. This is handy for hiding blemishes, such as pimples. It works by blending the colors within the circle. First, use the slider to adjust the circle size. Then click or drag the brush over the blemish. A single click works best for small areas.

Effects. Change your photo to black & white, or choose among four other color options. There are also three options here to frame your photo.

 Adjust. The editing tools in here are kinda like what you find in Enhance and Effects. But here, you can determine just how much you want the effect to affect your picture! *I just had to use those two words together! effect... affect... snicker.... I know...sorry... I'm easily amused!*

If you don't like your edits, click on Cancel, or from the menu bar Edit > Undo.

If you want the change to be permanent, click on Done.

Good Luck and Have Fun!

Keyboard Shortcuts 🍎

Keyboard shortcuts can be used in many applications.

Here are some of the most common keyboard shortcuts, the shortcuts you shouldn't do without!

For more shortcuts, go to www.apple.com. Click on Support. Beside "Search Support" type "keystroke shortcuts".

Keys must be pressed and held down at the same time to make the shortcut work.

The Command key is labeled ⌘ or with an Apple.

The Alt/Option key is labeled ⌥

⌘ S	Save
Shift ⌘ S	Save as
⌘ P	Print
⌘ W	Close window
⌥ ⌘ W	Close all windows
⌘ I	Show file information
⌘ Delete	Move to Trash
⌘ E	Eject
⌘ F	Find
⌘ Z	Undo
⌘ C	Copy
⌘ V	Paste
⌘ A	Select All
⌘ M	Minimize window
⌘ ?	Help Menu

Notes

_____

_____

_____

_____

_____

_____

_____

_____

_____

Remember...

Help is great!
Don't forget to use Help before you get frustrated.
You will always see Help along the menu bar
for any application you have open.

You will also find fabulous explanations and tutorials on
the Apple website under Support.
Search out mac101, it's terrific!

www.apple.com

Spotlight is Helpful!
Don't forget to use Spotlight
if you can't find something in your Mac.
Spotlight is the best at pointing things out!

Index

Index

Index

Index

Index

Index

Index

Index

Did I miss something you want in the index?

Write it down here!

_____

_____

_____

_____

_____

_____

_____

_____

_____

_____

_____

_____

_____

_____

_____

_____

_____

Notes

Hi I'm Louise, here's my story. I was so excited in 2002, when my parents got their first computer. My family and I were living on the East coast and they were in the West. Anything that would make the miles shrink between us was a good thing!

They knew zilch about computers, so right away I went to look for a book to get them going! Then I panicked. There was not a book on the shelves that spoke to them.

There was a lot of stress in their lives at that time. Dad had lung cancer and Mom, a retired nurse, wanted to be able to do some research on the internet. They needed to learn how to use the computer quickly and easily, so I started writing them notes. How-to notes with pictures of exactly what to do; "just do this" explanations.

The notes grew and friends started asking for copies. That's how the idea of forming them into a book came to be.

I brought the first draft of the book with me and my sons when we travelled home for March break in 2003. Dad was so proud of me, of what I had written. I think he knew this book would take me on a journey. That it would grow.

Dad passed away that April. I miss him, we all miss him. He was a man who brought joy with him and left optimism in his wake. He is the angel that guides me.

~~~

This is my third book in the My Parents computer book series, and the first for a Mac computer. I hope you will find it easy to follow and have fun learning to use your Mac!

To all my family and friends, thank you. I could not do this without your help and incredible support.

And thank you to you, for asking me to write it.